ATLANTIS
IN THE
AMAZON

"This is a long-overdue book by an authority on the Carlo Crespi collection and what it means to our understanding of the first travelers to the Americas, *long* before Columbus. Not only is the case made for Atlantis in the Amazon, but Wingate also shows how this collection sounds a clear warning that humanity's destructive ways are drawing us ever nearer to the same annihilation that wiped out this once thriving and advanced culture. Sadly, Wingate makes the case for the high probability that we are to go the way of Atlantis by continuing to use nuclear energy."

ROBERT R. HIERONIMUS, PH.D., AUTHOR OF
FOUNDING FATHERS, SECRET SOCIETIES AND
HOST OF 21STCENTURYRADIO.COM

"The controversial Crespi Collection is presented here by the man who personally examined its artifacts before they were confiscated by Ecuadoran authorities. Richard Wingate's photographs and descriptions of beautifully made objects representing Assyrian or Babylonian figures document the arrival of Near Eastern culture-bearers in South America nearly three thousand years ago."

FRANK JOSEPH, AUTHOR OF
ADVANCED CIVILIZATIONS OF PREHISTORIC AMERICA

ATLANTIS
IN THE
AMAZON

Lost Technologies
and the Secrets
of the Crespi Treasure

RICHARD WINGATE

Bear & Company
Rochester, Vermont • Toronto, Canada

Bear & Company
One Park Street
Rochester, Vermont 05767
www.BearandCompanyBooks.com

Text stock is SFI certified

Bear & Company is a division of Inner Traditions International

Library of Congress Cataloging-in-Publication Data

Wingate, Richard, 1933–
  Atlantis in the Amazon : lost technologies and the secrets of the Crespi treasure / Richard Wingate.
      p. cm.
  Includes bibliographical references and index.
  ISBN 978-1-59143-120-6 (pbk.)
  1. Atlantis (Legendary place) 2. Crespi, Carlos, 1891–1982—Ethnological collections. 3. Ecuador—Antiquities. I. Title.
  GN751.W568 2011
  398.23'4—dc22

                                                            2011007179

Printed and bound in the United States by Lake Book Manufacturing
The text stock is 100% SFI certified. The Sustainable Forestry Initiative® program promotes sustainable forest management.

10   9   8   7   6   5   4   3   2   1

Text design and layout by Virginia Scott Bowman
This book was typeset in Garamond Premier Pro with Garamond, Agenda, and Gill Sans used as display typefaces

To send correspondence to the author of this book, mail a first-class letter to the author c/o Inner Traditions • Bear & Company, One Park Street, Rochester, VT 05767, and we will forward the communication.

CONTENTS

Introduction   1

PART ONE
Evidence of an Ancient Civilization
Father Crespi's Treasure

1   Bimini Boogie   4

2   Atlantis in the Bahamas   10

3   First Visit to Crespi's Treasure   19

4   *Man, Whence, How, and Whither*   48

5   The Sting   58

6   Farewell, My Friend   67

7   Dinner Conversation: A Boiled Fish Surprise   69

PART TWO
The Misuse of Ancient Science and Technology
The Voluntary Stone Age

8   The Mysterious Disappearance of Percy Fawcett   74

9   Legends of Atlantis   79

10   The Panecillo Laser   86

11   The Powerful Wooden UFOs   92

12   The Mahabharata   96

13   Time and the Atomic Latte   103

14   The Doomsday Device   110

15   Rocket Attack   113

16   The Fimbul Winter   118

Conclusion   122

Appendix One. *Critias*   123

Appendix Two. *Timaeus*   135

Appendix Three. A Deeper Look at the   142
Crespi Collection of Cuenca, Ecuador,
By Warren Cook and Warren Dexter

Bibliography   161

Index   162

INTRODUCTION

THIS BOOK IS WRITTEN IN two parts. Part One begins with evidence of an ancient civilization in the Caribbean, which could have been part of the far-flung diaspora of Atlantis. It also tells the story of Father Carlo Crespi and the fabulous collection of ancient artifacts he gathered in the Jivaro headhunters' jungle near Macas in the Ecuadorian *selva* (rainforest). The chief of one tribe told him, "Now that we are Christians, the old oaths to our ancestors don't bind us any more, and I will take you to what we have been guarding for the ancestors." He led Padre Crespi, then a young Catholic missionary-anthropologist, to deep tunnels containing thousands of artifacts, loads of gold, and most amazing of all, technology from a previous lost civilization: steel-hard copper wheels and gears, aluminum "wallpaper," machinery of unknown usage, and tons of Assyrian, Babylonian, Cretan, and Aryan artifacts. The priest had money of his own from an inheritance, which he had wisely invested, and he was able to purchase much of the tunnel's contents. Without stretching the imagination too much, it is possible to believe these artifacts and the strange technology did indeed come from a now deliberately vanished scientific civilization. That someone hid this treasure is obvious. But what was the motive?

1

The second part of this book reveals that the "prehistoric" Hindu Aryans had science and technology and misused it. The misuse: a worldwide nuclear war, fought for world domination. The few survivors, in consensus, helped no doubt by a "green" police effort to eliminate all trace of technology and the horrible memory of radiation poisoning, which deliberately plunged us into the Stone Age. Except that this Stone Age was voluntary. The Hindu holy history books, such as the Mahabharata and Rig Veda, describe this war in great detail: the launching of nuclear weapons, the destruction of entire races of people, and the subsequent dismantling and concealing underground of all science and technology by enlightened kings. This hidden science is now emerging. This is its story.

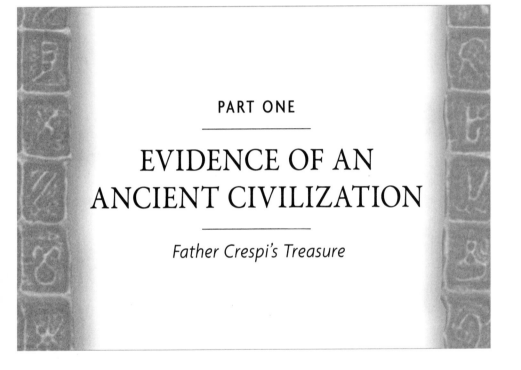

PART ONE

EVIDENCE OF AN ANCIENT CIVILIZATION

Father Crespi's Treasure

BIMINI BOOGIE

"HEY RICHAH, RICHAH, MON." Sgt. Rolle* of the Bimini Constabulary was pounding on my door. The clock said 6:00 a.m. I was trying to sleep off an exceptionally good night of jugging and jawing, so I rolled over and put the pillow over my head. The place was Jim Richardson's house next to his hotel, the Bimini Islands Yacht Club on the south island of Bimini in the Bahamas.

"Hey Richah, mon." I got up and opened the door a crack. There was the sergeant with four of his fellow officers. He was wearing his official uniform, dress whites, but the other police didn't have uniforms on, just outlandish party clothes; one of them, Leroy, was carrying a .22 rifle, while the sergeant had strapped on his large revolver, an English Webley .455. This was heavy—the Royal Bahamas Police Force follows the British tradition: no firearms unless it is really serious.

"Come on, Richah, get your boat. We got work to do. A crashed plane." I was almost alert by now. Michael Lopez, my stepson, staggered from another bedroom. We splashed cool water on our faces

---

*Not his real name.

and ran down to our little boat, a twenty-two-foot Sea Ray. I checked the gas; the tank was full. We were ready to go but no breakfast and no coffee. Damn! As we untied the boat and headed down the canal toward open water, the sergeant told me the story. A cargo plane had crashed in a fierce lightning storm in the night as it was taking off from the tiny Bimini Airport. It had to be a smuggler's plane, because the airport was officially closed at night. I hoped it wasn't filled with injured or drowned illegals on their way to a new life in the United States.

We stopped to tie on our thirteen-foot Boston Whaler outboard, then Mike gunned the Sea Ray out of the Bimini harbor and we headed for a World War II cargo plane. It sat with the fuselage barely showing above the water's surface, and its big fat tail jutted out of the water (figs. 1.1–1.3, pp. 5–7). You couldn't miss it. A fisherman had reported that a man was standing on the wing, but he was nowhere in sight. As we roared up to the plane we spotted another boat, which had been hidden from view by the airplane's huge tail. They gunned away fast, so we chased them with the sergeant holding his Webley revolver at the ready. They had a fast boat, but we were faster. When they saw they couldn't outrun us, they stopped. There were no weapons aboard, so the sergeant read them a lecture about running from the police. "We were just curious," the nervous fishermen from Ft. Lauderdale said lamely.

Fortunately, there were no illegal aliens, no bodies, just a cargo of Mexican marijuana, gasoline-soaked from a ruptured fuel tank. The plane was full of bales and bales of cargo. The sergeant had his men dive down and they began salvaging the cargo.

Policeman Leroy, wearing outrageous high-heeled platform shoes, stood on a bale of recovered pot clutching a single-shot .22 rifle while fiercely scanning the sky. His fellow officer said in a bantering tone, "Whatcha gonna doo wit dat little popgun, mon?"

"If dey come back, we be ready fo dem," he fiercely replied. Mike cracked a little sarcastic smile, but I liked the man; Officer Leroy was a fighter. "Put the gun in the boat and start bringin' up the stuff like the

Fig. 1.1. The Bahamas police recovering marijuana from a crashed World War II cargo plane hit by lightning during an electrical storm as it took off from Bimini airport, illegally, at night

Fig. 1.2. The tail of the sinking plane

Fig. 1.3. The author with the ill-fated cargo

rest o' the men," the sergeant said, gently, and then I knew why he was the sergeant.

An expensive, sport-fishing boat roared up, filled with young Bimini men. Just curious. The pilot yelled at me, "Hey Richah, I knew yoo wit de police. Yoo ain't lookin fo' 'Lantis," the captain yelled hostilely. The sergeant ordered them back to Bimini. The local Bahamians often made big money salvaging cargo from Latin America. The men demanded the film when the sergeant got back to Bimini that evening. "Dey put our pitchas up in de customs office," they angrily told the sergeant.

And again he answered gently, "I sent them to Nassau this afternoon. Ain't nothing gonna happen to them. You okay, man." The "captain" turned away from the sergeant, satisfied with Sergeant Rolle's word.

Back at the downed plane, the Coast Guard helicopter had completed an air search around the plane, and a crewman held up a handwritten sign for us. It simply said "Body," and beneath that crude message was an arrow pointing down. We drove to where the chopper hovered and saw a body floating about ten feet down in the crystal-clear water: it was a man. There was a big discussion in our boat about who was going to recover the corpse. No one wanted to until Leroy, the combative policeman, volunteered. The body was Edward Skene; his driver's license said he was twenty-five years old and from Boston, Massachusetts. Blood was oozing from his nose and ears. He had gotten banged around in the crash and probably drowned. I suspect his companion, the man who had been spotted on the downed plane's wing, must have tried to save him, and when death was obvious, cast him adrift as incriminating evidence.

The sergeant said, "Now look what has happened to him—his life cut off, and he was a young man." Sergeant Rolle's sympathy touched my heart, and I wondered if Edward Skene had left a sweetheart or wife and children, or perhaps a mom and dad back in Boston who would remember giving him a talking to about his reckless ways. Ah, Edward. Ah, Bimini!

We headed back to Bimini for breakfast—a steaming bowl of conch chowder and the long-delayed cup of coffee. The police put Edward Skene in the tiny jail, a blanket over his body, then filled the jail to the ceiling with the recovered eighty-pound bales and had to stash the overflow behind the jail. That's when the "fast-boat" crowd got their revenge on the "'Lantis-man."

That evening I went to bed early, and as local Bimini gossip told me the next day, two of the "fast-boat" crowd "borrowed" Michael's thirteen-foot Boston Whaler, stole a boatload of grass from behind the jail, threw in some spare gas, and tootled their way to Nassau, the Bahamian capital, a little more than a hundred and twenty miles away—open water all the way and a dangerous crossing at night in a thirteen-footer with no spare motor. The grass was sold and back they came, considerably happier.

We found out later that the mysterious "wing" man had been rescued by the Chalk company's commercial seaplane coming from

Fig. 1.4. Richard and Beatrice Wingate searching Bimini with radio metal detector

Nassau on its way to the United States. When he got to the States the rescued man apparently walked right through customs and immigration and got clean away.

One of the real problems with searching for Atlantis in the Bahamas is that generally the smugglers thought we were police, and the U.S. Coast Guard thought we were smugglers, and if the Bahamas Self Defense Force had captured our Boston Whaler full of stolen grass, it wouldn't have been nice for us. But we persisted.

ATLANTIS
IN THE BAHAMAS

JIM RICHARDSON SHOOK ME awake, "Rich, take a look at the instruments," he said, his voice tight with tension. "The damned things are going nuts." We were flying to Jim's flight center in Opa Locka, Florida, from the Exuma Cays, which are on the eastern edge of the Bahamas. We were west of Bimini.

Tired from scanning the flat, monotonously white sands of the Great Bahamas Bank while we searched for a prehistoric oasis, I had fallen asleep. Since the dazzling white sand must obviously have been a dry desert ten thousand years ago, before the world's ocean levels rose to drown it, we might find a spring, and around the spring an oasis. Suddenly there it was: a clearly defined oasis/spring apparently still flowing, and scattered about it were shapes under the sand (see fig. 2.1). Buildings?

We were searching for archaeological remains in the waters of a vast, shallow, flat mesa jutting up from the sea floor. Specifically, we were looking for the remains of a marble building that Jim's son Robbie had found, which, had it been in the Mediterranean, would definitely have been identified as an ancient Greek temple. However, in the Bahamas

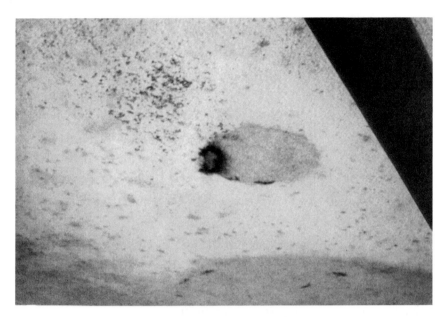

Fig. 2.1. Underwater oasis and building off the coast of West Bimini.
The object in the upper right is the strut of the airplane wing.

it was an *oopart* (out of place artifact) and had no business being there. Atlantis, perhaps?

Robbie had gathered thirty tons of this marble and had taken it to Nassau where it was installed in their small museum under the direction of Senator Doris Johnson, a Bahamian official who was minister of transport and had legal jurisdiction over ruins and wrecks.

Other parts of the marble, along with some peculiar granite, had been taken by barge to build part of the jetty off the coast of Miami Beach. We identified this granite as being ancient because of its irregular drill holes (see fig. 2.5).

And there it was: twenty miles north of Bimini under only twenty-two feet of water. On a return trip by boat, my stepson Mike and I were able to clear debris and many years of growth from the marble by using a homemade blower (shown in fig. 2.2). There were three wrecks scattered around the marble ruins. One was a wooden sailing ship carrying key-lock safes made in New York City. Another was an ancient

Spanish cargo vessel, which we identified because it was carrying tin ingots stamped with "La Mina Divina" (The Divine Mine), almost certainly from the rich Spanish tin mines of Bolivia, and almost certainly being transported to Spain to be mixed with copper and tin to cast bronze cannons or mixed with zinc to cast bronze. The third sunken ship, sinking sometime after ship number two, carried 1904 key-lock safes and was filled with marble blocks. Someone in recent times had been in the midst of salvaging the marble when the salvor's small ship, not more than fifty feet long, the hold filled with marble blocks, sank, quite likely in a storm, and sat on the rotten remains of the Spanish galleon. At least one person died in the wreck because a human knucklebone was plucked from a drilled hole in the marble. There was more marble lying loose around the wreck, enough to fill the hold of another ship. The marble building was a genuine artifact.

Quite likely the Spanish galleon and the key-lock safe ship sank in the ferocious hurricanes that plague the Caribbean. The relentless tides must

Fig. 2.2. Mike Lopez and Kenny Huertas fastening a "mailbox" sand duster to the propeller mount on our boat. We dusted the sand off the entire marble building in only a quick fifteen minutes. The propeller blast came out the bottom of the tube with truly awesome force.

Fig. 2.3. Pilot Jim Richardson rolling a drum of gas for our hi-tech Bimini refueling

Fig. 2.4. The marble temple after clearing the sand away

Fig. 2.5. Mike Lopez pointing to hand drilled, irregular sized holes in granite from a sunken building in the Bahamas and used in the Miami Beach jetty. The holes are not modern granite quarrying holes, which are machine drilled and uniform.

have moved the wrecks till they snagged on the marble ruins. Manson Valentine, a noted zoologist, had wood from the Spanish wreck tested at the University of Miami by carbon-14, which revealed the ship had been built between 1700 and 1800 CE. The key-lock safe ship was easily dated, for on the safe door the still-legible enameled letters read 1904.

The giant bronze pins from the Spanish galleon tin wreck had turned black, showing they possibly had been exposed to sulfur, for copper pins would have corroded into green. Hence we concluded that the tin wreck had landed on a sulfur spring flowing up under the marble building. Then it was time to nap. Jim's anxious voice woke me. The flight instruments were indeed acting nutty. Jim pointed to the ground-speed indicator needle, which tells the pilot how fast the plane is flying over the ground. The needle was gradually creeping down, yet we appeared to be moving faster than we ought. Jim's Cessna cruised at 140 mph, while the air-speed needle inched slowly up to 190 mph. I asked Jim if we were in a tailwind, but he pointed again to the ground-speed indicator, which hones in on a radio beacon on Bimini, now behind us, as we headed west toward Ft. Lauderdale. The display showed us that we were flying slow, white-knuckle slow, as the plane approached stall speed. Uh, oh! Jim, a veteran pilot (he flew a P51 Mustang against the Germans in World War II) admitted that he suddenly felt nervous. *That makes two of us,* I thought.

We exchanged serious glances as I reached into the backseat for the life jackets. If we survived the crash, would the coast guard get to us in time? While they searched for us, we would be floating north, carried by the Gulf Stream, legs dangling in the water, an enticing mouthful for one of the big sharks. An irrational surge of fear convinced me that somehow the sharks knew we didn't have a life raft. Then, to our relief, the instruments slowly, ever so slowly, went back to normal. We were picking up ground speed and gradually the air-speed indicator slowed to normal cruising speed. We were okay. Whatever had us was letting go.

Back at the flight center we discussed the peculiar "creature" that had grabbed us. Jim reminded me that crazy things were going on in the Bermuda Triangle, which includes the Bahamas islands. We've noticed our compass needle sometimes distorts crazily while flying over the Bahamas bank. Is there a logical explanation? A few people with vivid imaginations wondered if the sunken machinery of Atlantis is still functioning after all those years and affecting flight instruments.

A month passed, and we were once again flying from the Exuma Cays, where we had found two mysterious pillars still standing on two tiny, isolated cays. One column had what appeared to be a sundial at its base.

The drone of the Cessna's engine had, as usual, put me to sleep. Jim woke me and said, "The damned thing is doing it again." This time we were ready, and Jim banked the plane sharply. The wing dipped left, we banked, and a minute or two after Jim leveled the plane, the instruments slowly pointed back to normal. Whatever had grabbed us had let go. The explanation was that we had been in a freak wind and simply turned out of it. The prevailing wind that day was blowing in one direction, and what had us was a narrow bore, a pencil wind, blowing in the opposite direction. Meteorologists don't know about such winds. Pilots without a ground-speed indicator would fly into such a death bore and fly on at decreased speed until they ran out of gas. Is this what happened to the entire flight of U.S. Navy Avenger pilots that mysteriously disappeared while flying over the Bahamas? Possibly, but what about the whiteouts and compass deviations reported by numerous flyers? Is there a logical explanation? Perhaps. That question was partially answered one afternoon on Bimini by Junior, a friend who lived in a houseboat up in Porgy Town. He told me about strange rocks being dredged up by a local homeowner who was deepening and enlarging his dockage because he needed a deeper mooring. The hired bucket dredge was biting into the coral limestone and hitting hard rock, including chunks of granite, some blue-gray shale, and an extremely heavy black rock. Granite is a continental rock, and shale forms from freshwater clay, and neither should be on Bimini, which is all coral limestone down thousands of feet, according to established geologists. The black stone was definitely magnetite, a major iron ore. What was it doing under the limestone of Bimini harbor?

Naysayer geologists claim that any continental rock found in the Bahamas must be ship's ballast. To find out if it was ballast, I went to see Junior, a 250-pound, six-foot-tall native Bahamian teenager who had dug an eighty-pound rock out of the ground near the King's Highway. Junior pointed to streaks of purple running through the boulder of magnetite iron ore. Now we had two locations for the iron ore, and a few weeks later, Joe Granville brought us to another location. Joe, who pioneered underwater TV for oil-well pipeline inspection and made a bundle, brought back lab reports from Miami of a black sand collected on the Bahamas bank by free-diving record holder Jacques Mayol. The sample was magnetite, one of the major world sources for iron ore, and a large body of it might cause a compass to point off course. What about a peculiar greasy fog called the "Atlantis fog"? Suppose a pilot gets caught in a combination of pencil wind and the Atlantis fog while flying over a great deposit of magnetite. Thoroughly confused, the pilot flies on until he runs out of gas and crashes.

Later, back in Florida, we called Manson Valentine. Perhaps he had some thoughts on these peculiar pencil winds. Valentine, a maverick scientist who was ridiculed by his colleagues for believing there had been an Atlantis, had been studying the underwater "roadway" and other constructions that he and pilots Trig Adams and Bob Brush had discovered. "No," he said slowly shaking his head, "I've never heard of these strange winds. We'll have to go flying sometime and study them." Then he suddenly changed the subject. "Have you ever heard of the Crespi Collection?"

I had heard of it on an extended prospecting trip to the headwaters of the Amazon River system of Ecuador in 1963 but had never seen it. A local newspaper mentioned that a Catholic missionary priest named Carlo Crespi claimed that Egyptians had sailed up the Amazon River and colonized ancient Peru. His theory was substantiated by tons of artifacts he had recovered from deep tunnels in the rainforest of Ecuador. The museum housing the artifacts had mysteriously burned to the ground and, Crespi told a reporter for the Ecuadorian newspaper, *La Prensa Grafica,* some of his best artifacts had been lost in the fire. The museum had been filled with many golden objects and heavy copper and stone mechanical devices, along with what he believed to be Egyptian, Babylonian, and Assyrian artifacts. Popular opinion in Cuenca was that local leftists had set the fire to conceal a massive theft of the golden portion of the treasure. Since no puddles of molten gold were found in the ashes, that seemed like a plausible scenario.

Dr. Valentine suggested that I go to Ecuador and photograph the artifacts that had survived the fire. "Rich, take lots of pictures; what survived the fire might surprise you. There might be a connection to our Atlantis."

A few days later I flew to Cuenca to see Carlo Crespi and discover why professional anthropologists and archaeologists called him a buffoon, and I was delighted to find that he was anything but. In fact, he had multiple anti-buffoon degrees from universities in Italy, including one in anthropology and doctorates in engineering and music. He was an extremely well-educated man with a salty indifference to "expert" opinions. I knew I would like him.

FIRST VISIT
TO CRESPI'S TREASURE

"I LOVE THAT MAN," my companion said with a beautiful smile, "the peoples [*sic*] around here think he is a saint." We were on our way to a storehouse of marvels I had heard described by Manson Valentine in Miami, just two days before. "That man" was Carlo Crespi—jungle missionary, priest of the Maria Auxiliadora Church, anthropologist, holder of numerous doctorates, explorer, filmmaker, and discoverer of an extraordinary archaeological treasure.

My companion was travel agent Cecelia de Eguez, who was my translator and one of Father Crespi's many devoted friends. The town we were in was Cuenca, eight-thousand-feet high in the Andes Mountains of Ecuador.

When we arrived at the church, Father Crespi's bent, aged figure strode quickly out to meet us with a lot of zip for an eighty-six-year-old man. "Cecelia!" he exclaimed, his eyes widening with pleasure. "When are you going to bring me a little one to baptize?" Cecelia blushed and introduced us with the affection due her family priest.

Crespi shook my hand vigorously. "So, you're the archaeologist, eh?" he asked, a sly smile twinkling his pale-blue eyes. Cecelia translated the wry greeting. "Not an archaeologist, an investigator and photographer, and a person who, knowing of your collection, has great respect for your work."

"Ah," the priest said, "enough flattery, let's take a look." Without ceremony, he forced a key into an ancient rusty padlock and opened the rickety door to his shed. He touched two bare wires together and a watery yellow light glimmered. Father Crespi was smiling like a man with a remarkable secret.

I was astonished at his huge collection of artifacts. Stacked against one wall were seven-foot-tall golden mummy cases in the quasi-Egyptian style with a fire-blackened finish.

Fig. 3.1. The author with fire-blackened golden sarcophagus centerpiece in the Egyptian style. Photo by Kurt Lowenstein.

Fig. 3.2. An aluminum ark: hidden from sight are genuine gold rings to insert carrying poles. Animals marching up to a sun disc suggest this genuine artifact is pre-Hebrew.

Fig. 3.3. Semite with oxidized green copper patina. The statue resembles painter Marc Chagall's *The King*.

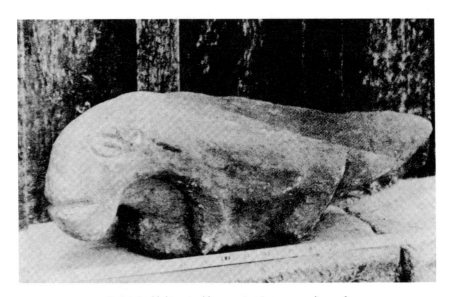

Fig. 3.4. Could this animal be an extinct Lystrosaurus dinosaur?

Fig. 3.5. A plaque of unknown metal. Are we looking at pre-Hebrew Adam and Eve? The man displays the
Atlantean (Neanderthal?) jutting jaw and has the ubiquitous sperm cells carved on his thigh. Between him
and the woman sits a devilish figure fondling a serpent. The woman appears to be the Goddess Athena,
protector of the Greeks, and above her head is her sacred full-moon owl. She carries a spear and wears a
Masonic apron. The woman was a Mason, before male gods usurped feminine power.

There were a few sets of what appeared to be gleaming golden suits of Incan parade armor alongside golden Chaldean-style helmets and golden plaques inscribed with a linear alphabet, later identified as proto-Phoenician by professor Barry Fell.

Fig. 3.6. Unidentified metal, Phoenician? Ancient writers said that Phoenician was the prime language of Atlantis.

Fig. 3.7. The ark; perhaps the figure on right is an extinct five-toed llama?

Piled haphazardly on the floor were rich-red copper shields, much pottery, sheets and rolls of silver-colored metal, rolls of golden sheet metal, strange gears and wheels, and peculiar brass pipes with no threading. Scattered among the gold were plaques depicting dinosaurs. *King Midas's treasure in a rainforest junk pile,* I thought.

The priest pointed to a gray metal ark piled on top of peculiar machines of unknown usage. The ark had golden rings fastened on the sides, obviously to accommodate poles that slipped in for carrying; and it had a hinged door (see fig. 3.2 on page 21). The decorative animal figures on this ark—an elephant, a llama, and most puzzling, a dinosaur, perhaps a Brontosaurus—were parading upward toward a metal cutout sun disk (fig. 3.7). Shoved carelessly under piles of other artifacts in a dark corner of the shed were stone and copper mechanical devices with circular stonerollers.

Stone grinding mills, wheeled and geared, but in design unlike anything used by the Spanish, lay partly buried and covered in spider webs. Rolls of intricately repoussé sheet metal, every inch decorated with cartoon figures, were stacked against the walls.

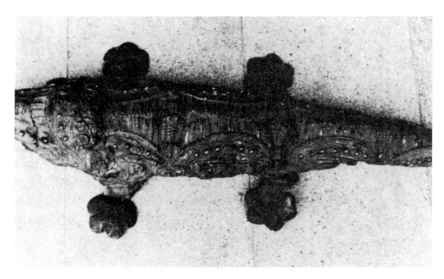

Fig. 3.8. A two-foot-long golden lizard with ruby-colored gemstone eyes

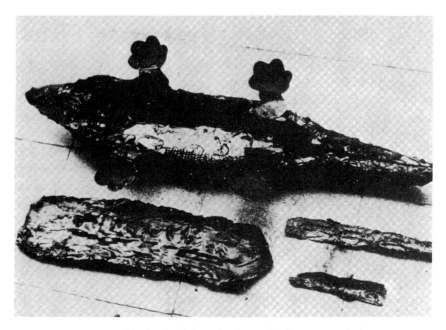

Fig. 3.9. A golden lizard with the underside coated with tar to give it body

Fig. 3.10. A dinosaur with sperm-cell decorations

Fig. 3.11. A sheet of unidentified metal. Hierophant on throne observing a crude-looking man with spear and fighting dogs attacking a prehistoric crocodilian.

Fig. 3.12. A "charming" gold,
fire-blackened figure

Fig. 3.13. An elephant plaque of
golden-colored stone. Barry Fell
translated this plaque. He thought
it should read, "The elephant that
supports the world and causes it
to shake." This could be describing
a scientific principle, the concept
of "zero point." Ancient Hindu
science believed the earth and all
heavenly bodies are held in place
by a zero point, or neutral center.

Fig. 3.14. A copper plaque of a woman who was perhaps meant to represent Mother Earth.

The rolls of sheet metal were seven and eight feet tall and were made from three-foot-wide pieces artfully riveted together with tiny, delicate rivets to make rolls that were ten- to fifteen-feet long. There were woven copper rectangles suggesting heat-exchange devices, but decorated with brass air pipes. Father Flores-Haro, his devoted pupil, told anthropologist Warren Cook that after an exhausting day, the old priest would spend two or three hours studying books on anthropology and archaeology. His native suppliers cut up rolls of metallic "wallpaper" ripped from the walls of buildings in the rain forest to forge more saleable artifacts—saleable only to the priest, that is—such as the metal statue with modern false teeth, a laughable real-fake, for the sheet metal body of the statue was the real wallpaper "and the teeth were made in a local dental lab" (see fig. 3.16 on page 30).

Fig. 3.15. This aluminum "wallpaper" is made from cold-rolled pure aluminum. The grains of metal are elongated and flat. To buy this kind of metal today you have to special order it. The ancient fabricators rolled it into three-foot-wide strips, fastened into fifteen- to thirty-foot sheets by tiny, delicate aluminum rivets. Tear holes at top suggest it was ripped from walls.

Crespi was a shrewd psychologist. Archaeologists just shake their heads when they discover that he knowingly bought fakes, yet his generous and open attitude endeared him to his beloved Indian friends. This attitude kept the artifacts flowing, and much in his collection is obviously real and fantastic.

In fact, his attitude and sharp eye brought him one of the finest collections of Ecuadorian pottery and artifacts in the country, as noted by the archaeologists who supervised the looting of his rickety storage sheds. It seems he had a keen eye for beauty.

His jungle diggers once brought him fifty-two bronze plaques of such great beauty and superb workmanship that a scientist at Baltimore's Walters Art Gallery, whom I visited later in 1977, exclaimed, "That is the most beautiful Nisroch figure I have ever seen."

What about the gold? Carelessly leaning against one wall was a roll of untarnished yellow wall covering, similar to the other aluminum sheet metal, except, of course, the metal was gold, as shown in plate 4.

Yet at times he paid huge sums. Flores-Haro tells of Crespi's paying five and ten thousand dollars per piece—if the article was large or made of gold.

Crespi told Flores-Haro that his father had left him a large inheritance, which he invested in Spanish colonial paintings. Using his church connections, he resold them in Europe and made a mint of money. He

Fig. 3.16. Metallic real-fake with modern dentures made in a lab in Cuenca. The ebony carving on the right is genuine Pacific Oceanic art.

needed lots of money to finance the trade school, and every day he fed a nourishing lunch to his two thousand pupils and supported hundreds of poor widows with children.

Then Carlo Crespi showed me a few dozen bronze plaques, his favorite pieces, lifted from a pile of about fifty or more. He let out a little cry of joy when he smilingly displayed them. There was an unmistakable royal Egyptian woman, a Nisroch, an Assyrian sacred

Fig. 3.17. A plaque of copper material: Aryan-Caucasian man with European features

Fig. 3.18. Ten copper-based plaques that Carlo Crespi was very fond of.
The remaining forty-two plaques have disappeared.

five-legged bull, and one of the plaques bore the image of a Caucasian
man writing linear script with a quill pen. Linear script? A quill
pen?

The archaeology was tumbled about in two sheds off the courtyard and also stacked in side rooms of the church. Crespi had once
had everything stored in an orderly fashion in a museum in his nearby
school, but after a fire destroyed his best artifacts, what survived was

Fig. 3.19. A bronze plaque of a giant. The severed head on the pole is half the giant's size. Perhaps the image of Goliath?

Fig. 3.20. An Aryan-Caucasian man. "David" holding a severed head with a dent in its forehead from David's sling stone. The pre-Hebrew Goliath story.

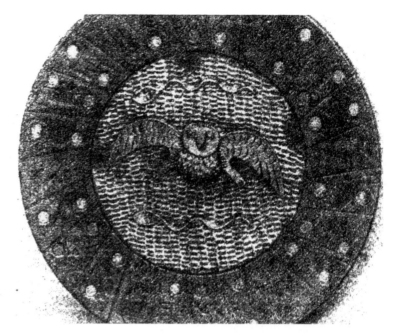

Fig. 3.21. Model T clutch plate (probably foisted on the priest in his old age)

Fig. 3.22. Segundo, Father Crespi's devoted worker, unrolls strips of unidentified metal.

Fig. 3.23. A playful Oswaldo Eguez and a smiling Father Crespi

brought to his church and jammed casually into the shed and a few empty rooms.

The genial priest let me take photographs. "As many as you like," he said. Most museums guard their treasures from casual photographers, so his open generosity won me over. Lack of space inside forced me to set up my tripod and camera in the outer courtyard. The priest himself brought the artifacts into the sun. Hours passed, and the usual afternoon equatorial rain began. At this point Crespi was getting tired, so we quit for the day. I had exposed more than ten rolls of film, taken more than three hundred pictures, and had only touched the edge of his huge pile. "Please come back tomorrow," Crespi said, "and bring the little one." He smilingly pointed to Cecelia.

The next day Cecelia, her husband Oswaldo, and her brother-in-law Jorge arrived to help. They cheerfully carried the strange stuff out into

Fig. 3.24. Pacific Ocean ebony carvings with genuine discolored gold headbands

the sunlit courtyard and were as amazed as I at the richness and beauty of many pieces, such as the yard-long golden lizard with red gemstone eyes shown in figures 3.8 and 3.9 (page 25).

"Are those stones in the eyes rubies?" Oswaldo asked. "I don't know," I replied, "but each one seems to be about thirteen to fourteen carats, and they have a lovely violet background color. They could be rubies; if they are, they are worth a fortune." The golden lizard was made of thin hammered gold, and its inside was coated with tar to give it body. Here,

Fig. 3.25. An Easter Island–style figure establishing
connection between Ecuador and Easter Island, which
is over one thousand miles west in the Pacific

then, was the secret of the Incan life-sized golden statues reported by
the Spanish: they were hollow.

I again took hundreds of photos, the afternoon rain began on
schedule, and then it was time to quit. The priest knew I had to fly
out the next day, and he shyly asked me to bring the photos back with
me the next time I came. He said wistfully that many people had come
to take photos but nobody, nobody ever brought any back to him. I
gave him a sincere promise.

Fig. 3.26. A maze on polished Diorite stone. This maze would be at home on ancient Crete. It describes a perfect Minoan-Cretan Mediterranean sacred labyrinth and is identical to one scratched on the wall of Lucretius's house in volcano-buried Pompeii.

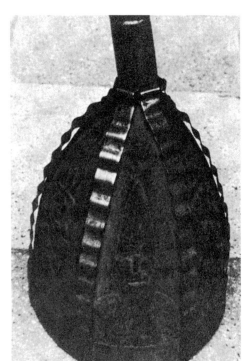

Fig. 3.27. A heavy, red copper crown decorated and held together by gold frame. Pictured on front is a bearded magician.

Fig. 3.28. Carlo Crespi with a statue of Eve and the serpent

Fig. 3.29. Bronze calendar disk identified by J. Manson Valentine, Ph.D.

Fig. 3.30. A charming figure cuddling a dolphin

Fig. 3.31. Unidentified metal figure with wings and a radiating box on its chest

Fig. 3.32. Figure with semi-precious carbuncle in its navel

Fig. 3.33. Two objects of intricately woven copper strips. They could be heat exchangers, but the one on the right is decorated with a fake figure. However, the piece on left is decorated with genuine high-pressure gas pipes with a thick wall and no threading. Objects are not modern and are classified as real-fake.

Fig. 3.34. A collection of real and fake helmets. All are constructed with real, ancient metal.

Fig. 3.35. Unidentified sheet metal of a smiling fish face with dinosaur on crown

Fig. 3.36. A bronze-colored Hierophant plaque (one of fifty-six). Notice the clerk is shown writing the proto-north Semitic language with a quill pen in a surprisingly modern looking book.

Fig. 3.37. This green patina copper shield is decorated with gold and sperm cells.

Fig. 3.38. An olive oil can that is considered a "fake" artifact

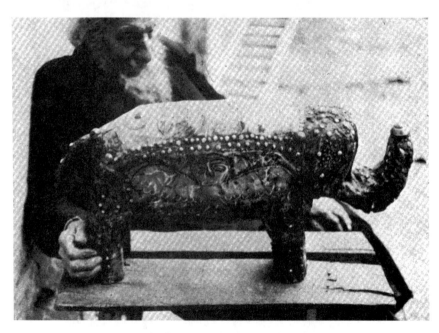

Fig. 3.39. Another fake decorated with modern brass thumbtacks

Fig. 3.40. An obvious fake artifact. (Charlie Brown?)

Fig. 3.41. Assyrian, five-legged bull-man. Compare to Neo-Assyrian human-headed winged bull (lamassu) dated 883–859 BCE in the Metropolitan Museum of Art, New York City. Photo courtesy of Wayne N. May, *Ancient American* magazine.

Fig. 3.42. Carlo Crespi displaying his collection of fine quality paintings.
Photo courtesy *Ancient American* magazine, Wayne N. May.

A warm good-bye to the Eguez family and an *abrazo* (hug) from my new friend Carlo Crespi ended the day. My plan was to fly straight to Baltimore to show the pictures to the Middle Eastern antiquities experts at the Walters Art Gallery (now the Walters Art Museum). I knew they had one of the finest Assyrian Nisroch marble bas-reliefs in the world, and their knowledge of the ancient Middle East was superb. Perhaps they would shed some light on the Crespi artifacts and the puzzle of their being found in tunnels in the Amazon rain forest.

A week later I was at the Walters with some of the photos. I presented a stunning eight-by-ten of the Assyrian Nisroch figure first.

"That is one of the most beautiful Nisrochs I have ever seen," said one of the archaeologists. "Where did you get the picture?" I told him I'd taken it and showed them photos of an Assyrian five-legged bull. "Superb," another said, "where did you get these photos?" Again, "I took them." Then they oohed and aahed, and a few minutes later came the same question, "Where did you get these marvelous photos?" Once again, "I took the photos."

Silence fell on the room, and they looked at me with quizzical expressions on their faces. "Did you say *took* the photos? *Where* did you take the photos?" I answered, "In the Roman Catholic Church of Maria Auxiliadora in Cuenca, Ecuador. The collector is Padre Carlo Crespi."

Then came the sharp reply: "It's all fake, fake, fake. Everybody knows the Assyrians and Egyptians didn't sail up the Amazon." Almost as if they had been wired, all three archaeologists got up in unison with the senior scientist and headed for the door. On the way out one of them said to me, "We don't believe in the diffusion of culture. The oceans are barriers, not highways. We simply don't," he repeated. "It's all fake, very definitely fake."

4

MAN, WHENCE,
HOW, AND WHITHER

ANNIE BESANT WIPED TEARS from her eyes and almost turned away from the foul sight of a stricken teenage match-factory girl. The girl was suffering, suffering horribly, from "fossy jaw," a deteriorating disease that rots the jawbone and invariably leads to a painful death. The fossy jaw was caused by yellow phosphorus being absorbed through her skin. At the factory, the girl dipped wooden matchsticks into the chemical witch's potion that coated the matchstick head. Because the dying girl was too sick to work now, even her tiny salary of a few desperately needed shillings per week was about to vanish.

"Could Mrs. Besant help us?" asked the girl's blind, poverty-stricken mother whose husband had deserted her. Annie would help, and she resolved to fight—to fight for all the exploited children in all the dangerous and soul-numbing factories in all of eighteenth-century Great Britain. After making arrangements for the child's care and the mother's relief, she set to work.

Annie teamed with newsman Herbert Burrows, another activist, and attacked the child labor system. Burrows and Besant were helped by a poem that roused decent British emotions, written by Sarah Norcliffe Cleghorn.

> *The golf links lie so near the mill*
> *That almost every day*
> *The laboring children can look out from work*
> *And see the men at play.*
>   "THE GOLF LINKS"

She began by leading the impoverished street sellers in a strike against the owners, which was brought to a successful conclusion. Eventually the British outlawed all child labor.

Besant went on the attack for social causes, speaking out eloquently; her friend and collaborator, the famous Irish writer George Bernard Shaw, said of her, "She is the world's most eloquent orator." Annie Besant took up all the unpopular causes in England and the world. She opposed the British invasion of Afghanistan in 1873. Yes, they were at it even then. She spoke out for India's independence from British rule, which got her jailed for a while, and when released she was elected president of the Indian National Congress. She is loved in India even today, where they still sing her praises with the lovely song, "Devi Vasanti" (Besant the Angel).

When Besant's spiritual teacher, a mahatma, Koot Hoomi, sent for her to visit him and have her brow chakra ("third eye") opened, she dropped everything and went to his headquarters in Kashmir, in the lovely hill and lake country of northern India. Koot Hoomi put her through rigorous training. For Besant, opening her brow chakra center was relatively easy; the tough part was learning to see clearly and understand the phenomenon revealed by other dimensions. Proof that she learned well is in the book, *Occult Chemistry,* in which her colleague, Bishop Charles Webster Leadbeater, also trained by Koot Hoomi, assisted. [Theosophical Society] Elwood Cook, a Baltimore psychologist, showed *Occult Chemistry* to his chemistry professor, who borrowed the book and spent a full weekend studying it. The professor told Cook he was convinced the writers had indeed actually seen the atom.

Koot Hoomi took Besant to see the CEO of the Brotherhood and Sisterhood of the Saints, and the maha chohan, as he is called, told Besant he wanted a history of the world written. It would explain "man, whence, how, and whither," and would trace our history back to the planets we were brought from (in great spaceships) and take us up to the year 2600 CE.

The English were just getting into steam engines and bicycles in 1913 when the book was published. "Nonsense, pure science fantasy," Besant's critics snorted in rage.

Surprisingly, much of Annie Besant's strange story has since been validated by real proof. For instance, she spoke of "the universal force" supplying the new world with free, nonpolluting power, and today there are actual working models busily pumping out the universal force, spinning away around the world, as tiny bands of dedicated, endangered-species inventors successfully experiment with zero-point free energy.

In her 1913 book, *Man, Whence, How, and Whither,* Besant mentions plans by "the brotherhood" to release wireless transmission of electricity as an interim step to get us accustomed to relatively free electricity when the worldwide tidal flows and moving waters are harnessed. Nikola Tesla was their chosen person, as he had already given us alternating current. Tesla successfully pumped juice into the ground and collected it as it circled the earth, surfing standing waves with practically no loss of energy through friction. Wireless transmission was a reality.

J. P. Morgan, the banking giant, refused to invest in Tesla's invention, saying, "If some little African can get my electricity by driving an iron rod into the ground, where is the profit for me?" Consequently, with Morgan's refusal, no one else dared lend Tesla the money, and Tesla's wireless transmission was put on the shelf. Besant's prophecy, like all prophecy, wasn't written in stone; it bowed to the human will—the will to greed in this case. As the Communion of Ascended Saints tells us, "The law is firm. We are allowed to offer ideas, plans, and suggestions, yes, and especially encouragement, but the law does not allow us to use force, for this would interfere with the very basis of cosmic purpose: freedom. Freedom to make mistakes and freedom to correct those mistakes, freedom to evolve, consequently freedom to increasingly express the magnificent universe that is within each of us." But this prophecy relating to Tesla verifies Annie Besant and her talents, so when she takes us back to Atlantis in Peru, the more adventurous among us might be tempted to think she was indeed seeing clearly.

The following brief excerpts are from her book, *Man, Whence, How, and Whither,* from the section, "Atlantis in Peru, 12,000 BC."

Religion: The most prominent characteristic of the religion was its joyousness. Grief or sorrow of any kind was held to be absolutely wicked and ungrateful, since it was taught that the Deity wished to see His children happy, and would Himself be grieved if He saw them grieving. Death was regarded not as an occasion for mourning, but rather for a kind of solemn and reverent joy, because the Great Spirit had accounted another of His children to approach nearer to Himself. Suicide, on the other hand, was, in pursuance of the same idea, regarded with the utmost horror as an act of the grossest presumption; the man who committed suicide thrust himself uninvited into higher realms for which he was not yet judged fit by the only authority who possessed the requisite knowledge to decide the question. But indeed, at the time of which we are writing, suicide was practically unknown, for the people as a whole were a most contented race. One of the most prominent theories was that all light and life and power came from the sun, a theory that is fully borne out by the discoveries of modern science.

Machinery: They had achieved considerable advances also in the construction and use of machinery, though most of it was simpler and rougher than ours, and they had nothing like the extreme accuracy in the fitting together of minute parts, which is so prominent a characteristic of modern work. [Plate 9 shows an example of such a piece of ancient machinery.]

On the other hand, though their machinery was often large and cumbrous, it was effective, and apparently not at all liable to get out of order, like the extremely hard copper wheel. This copper wheel is proof of exotic technology from the past. It won't flatten and become elliptical at high speeds. It is harder than we can make copper today. They had evidently some knowledge of hydraulics also, for many of their machines were worked by hydraulic pressure.

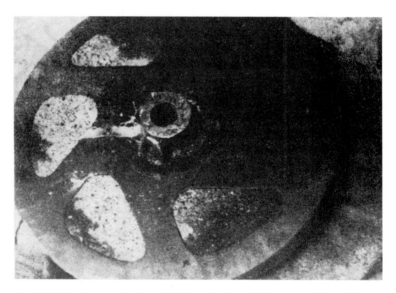

Fig. 4.1. Steel-hard copper wheel so well designed that it won't flatten out and lose efficiency at high speeds as modern wheels do

There was a good deal of scientific knowledge among them, but all of their science was of a severely practical kind. They had no sort of idea of such an abstract study of science as exists among ourselves.

Adhesive: . . . but they generally trusted entirely to the powerful adhesive, which they used in place of mortar . . . and poured in their "mortar" in a hot and fluid condition. Minute as were the crevices between the stones, this fluid found and filled them, and when it cooled it set like flint, which indeed, it closely resembled.

Fig. 4.2. An ancient wall in Cuenca, Ecuador. It is still standing even after a Spanish flour mill built around it had tumbled. This wall was standing, as part of an Incan palace, when the Spanish invaded.

They cut and fitted the enormous blocks of stone with the greatest accuracy, so that the joint was barely perceptible; then they plastered the outside of each juncture with clay, and then poured in their "glue" in a hot and fluid condition. The clay was then scraped off the outside and the wall was complete, and [if] after the lapse of centuries a crack in the masonry ever made its appearance, it was certainly not at any of the joints, for they were stronger than even the stone itself.

El Molino, the wall in Cuenca, was part of a mill built by the Spanish to grind wheat into flour; the builders used this ancient standing wall as part of the mill's construction. Ecuador's frequent earthquakes shook down the Spanish flour mill surrounding it, but the older Atlantean(?) wall still stands, as shown in fig. 4.3. (Clearly the ancient Atlanteans knew a lot about cement.)

The constituency of the cement is similar to that holding together

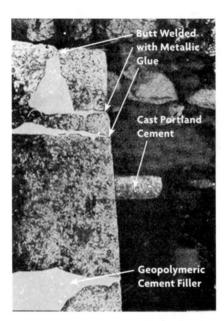

Fig. 4.3. The same wall (fig. 4.2) from the top, looking down. It is glued together with the ubiquitous iron cement, which the author has discovered in the Americas. This wall is proof of ancient high technology.

Fig. 4.4. Inca Pirca in Ecuador. Walls are built with the same iron cement found on the Cuenca wall.

a wall in Iraq dated at 4000 BCE, rediscovered by a chemist named Joseph Davidovits. He patented his discovery—flexible cement.

The ubiquitous glue was also recovered from a shattered pyramid in the Mojave Desert of California by music producer Cory Wade (figs 4.4, 4.5).

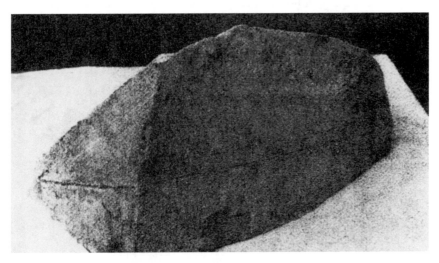

Fig. 4.5. Glued building block from the shattered, partially melted sixty-foot-high pyramid in the Mojave Desert. The iron glue holds the rock so tightly that, as Annie Besant stated, the rock broke off and the glue remained holding.

And on the other side of the Atlantic, a large and colorful Italian explorer named Belzoni discovered the facing stones at the bottom of the pyramid of Giza were cemented together with a one-fiftieth of an inch layer "of very tenacious cement." Recent photos also show great slabs of glue high up in the same pyramid. Here is our Atlantean adhesive described by Besant, on a structure in Egypt, which she said was another colony of Atlantis. The colony theory explains a sudden explosive culture like that in Mesopotamia (Iraq), which suddenly sprung out of nowhere, fully developed. Its sudden appearance puzzles archaeologists to this day. Can we chalk up another win for Annie Besant?

Imagine a giant geodesic dome of mortise and tenon, cast-marble blocks fitted together and then glued with this magnificent Atlantean glue. No need for expensive steel framework—the building is held together by its own monocoque (eggshell) earthquake-proof structure. This could be the housing for the new world now taking shape from our disintegrating old one. Buckminster "Buckyballs" Fuller would have danced with joy.*

Wallpaper: ". . . all houses of any consideration had their walls lined with some kind of metal, just as ours are now papered, but only the palaces of the king and chief governors were lined with pure gold like the temples; for the ordinary folk, all kinds of beautiful and service-able alloys were available and rich effects were produced at compara-tively little cost." [Two rolls were standing upright in Crespi's shed and the golden roll was stacked carelessly in a side storeroom.] These rolls are seven- to eight-feet high, are cold rolled and made from three-foot wide sheets, artfully riveted together with tiny, delicate rivets. The usual metal is aluminum, metallurgically pure, and the grains of metal seen under a microscope are long and thin, indicating they had been cold rolled. [Plate 4 shows some examples of these rolls.]

Curious sweetmeat: The potato and yam were cultivated and maize, rice, and milk in various combinations entered largely into their diet. They had, however, one curious and highly artificial food, which might have been called their staff of life—functioning some-what as bread does for us—as the principle foundation of most of their meals. The basis of this was maize flour, but various chemical constituents were mixed with it and the resultant subjected to enor-mous pressure, so that it came out at the end of the operation as a hard and highly concentrated cake. Its components were carefully arranged in order to contain within itself everything that was neces-sary for perfect nutrition in the smallest possible compass, and the experiment was so far successful that a tiny slice of it made sufficient provision for a whole day.

The simplest method of taking it was to suck it slowly like a loz-

---

*Buckminster Fuller invented a self-supporting geodesic dome, which became the namesake for a new generation of carbon compounds with a similar structure called fullerenes.

enge, but if time permitted it could be boiled or cooked in various ways, and the varieties of flavor were indicated by different colors. A pink cake was flavored with pomegranate, a blue with vanilla, a yellow with orange, a pink-and-white striped one with guava, and so on. This curiously compressed sweetmeat was the staple food and large numbers of people took nothing else, even though there were plenty of other dishes from which to select. It was manufactured in such enormous quantities that were exceedingly affordable.

Comparisons: The physical life with all its surroundings was better managed than, so far as we know, it has been since. The opportunities for unselfish work and devotion to duty, which were offered to the governing class, have perhaps never been surpassed. We are as yet a comparatively young race of Caucasians, whereas that which we have been examining was one of the most glorious offshoots of a race that had long since passed its prime. We are passing now, because of our ignorance, through a period of trial, storm, and stress, but out of it we too shall, in time, when we have developed a little common sense, emerge into a season of rest and success, and when that time comes to us it ought to reach, by the laws of evolution, an even higher level than theirs.

The ancient Hindus' voluminous writings on science, technology, and history are finally getting some serious Western attention. Obviously Eurocentric racial arrogance has kept the West from even reading the Indian cyclic view of evolution. This view answers more questions than it raises, while elegantly bridging the seeming dichotomy between science and religion. Annie Besant and her teachers simply reject the modern linear view of evolution with its gaps and contradictions and substitute ancient Hindu thought that evolution is simply the universe getting to know itself. This knowing occurs by ordered stages, while it is partly guided by an all-seeing brother- and sisterhood of good men and women who, through love, discipline, joy, and sacrifice have attained perfection. Men and women, out of love, assist us as far as we allow them. We are not facing the "brave new world" alone.

THE STING

THIS VERSION OF EVENTS was told to me by Hector Terranova, a Colombian, and I can vouch for Hector's character; he is truthful, and he was on the scene interviewing the church workers within a week after Crespi's death. Hector interviewed the church's employees, taxi drivers, backhoe operators (who buried the sheet metal in a twelve-foot-deep trench), and the night watchman, who was a particularly good source because he was outraged at the "sequestration" of Father Crespi and believed the shock killed his beloved priest.

The other source of information was an article by anthropologist Warren Cook and Warren Dexter. The facts are, well, the facts (see appendix 3).

The canvas-covered army truck eased quietly to the front door of the Church of Maria Auxiliadora (Mary Our Helper) in the beautiful Spanish colonial town of Cuenca. The soldiers got out and lined up before their officer, a white-skinned, thin, rosy-cheeked Spaniard with a pencil-thin mustache and jet-black hair and eyes. The two soldiers who snapped to attention before him were shorter and stockier and much darker. Their hair was thick and black and with their steel combat helmets on, you couldn't tell that they combed it straight back, Indian style.

Plate 1. Copper-based plaque.
Are we looking at a tax collector?

Plate 2. A golden plaque of Semite and 56-letter astronomical/
astrological tablet. Look for the bull, symbol of Taurus, in the fourth
row from the bottom, second from the right.

Plate 3. Thin gold ceremonial armor and
golden crown. The large copper-based
mitre is decorated with a few circles of
gold. Photo courtesy of Wayne N. May,
publisher of *Ancient American* magazine.

Plate 5. A gold plate identified by Professor Barry Fell as proto-Phoenician. Fell was fired from his teaching position for challenging the linguistic and archaeological establishment. He insisted ancient authors mentioned the Phoenicians got their language from a sunken continent.

Plate 4. Unidentified metal sheets. In the center, a roll of gold sheeting.

Plate 6. A golden decorative wall hanging, Notice the tiny holes in the bottom left for gold wire holding tassels. This decorative piece might have hung in someone's living room. Notice the morose half-animal, genetic mal-engineering creatures staring out at us.

Plate 7. An Atlantean priestess (or royal woman) gold plaque held by Carlo Crespi

Plate 8. Thin gold headpiece (left) and heavy gold crown (right).
The crown resembles King Comus of the European Mardi Gras festival.

Plate 9. Mechanical device of unknown function found in Crespi's shed

Plate 10. The author with Carlo Crespi. Father Crespi is holding the figure shown in more detail in plate 7. The author is holding a gold plaque of an Assyrian Nisroch or Assyr figure and a gold headpiece. Photo by Kurt Lowenstein.

Plate 11. Copper alphabet tablets. The tablet on top left shows happy faces at the end of each line of letters, no doubt a school tablet with a sixty-letter alphabet. This tablet displays programmed learning, a very sophisticated teaching technique. Barry Fell identified the tablet on the left as Proto-Phoenician. The tablet on the right pertains to algebra.

Plate 12. An Assyrian Nisroch copper-based plaque

Plate 13. Annie Besant described the original Atlanteans as having prognathous (jutting) jaws. The reverse side is shown in plate 14.

Plate 14. This copper plaque (the reverse side of plate 13) has a close resemblance to a Fibonacci spiral—the ratio by which all life unfolds.

Plate 15. Carlo Crespi holding a bronze-colored crescent moon

Plate 16. A heavy gold plaque. Photo courtesy of Wayne N. May, *Ancient American* magazine.

Plate 17. Rear of a modern bass viol. The metal is genuine bronze-colored wall covering. This one qualifies as a real-fake. Photo courtesy of Wayne N. May, *Ancient American* magazine.

Plate 18. Anthropology student Kurt Lowenstein holding a golden sheet metal column

Plate 19. J. Golden Barton, an early visitor to Crespi's museum, is holding a golden sheet and wearing a ceremonial golden helmet.

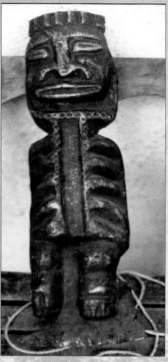

Plate 20. Heavy gold statue. Photo courtesy of Wayne N. May, *Ancient American* magazine.

Plate 21. Copper-based, heavy cast plaque. Note his tic-tac-toe ceremonial apron. The pavement displays perspective and a sacerdotal circular alphabet. His face is Caucasian. Photo courtesy of Wayne N. May, *Ancient American* magazine.

Plate 22. Bronze plaque. Man giving the Masonic high sign. Photo courtesy of Wayne N. May, *Ancient American* magazine.

The officer spoke. "Boys, we are here to see that nobody gets hurt, especially the old priest. Throw back the bolts of your rifles, let's take a look." Satisfied the rifles were empty, he asked if anybody was carrying ammunition. "No, *jefe*," (chief) they said in unison. Then Teniente (lieutenant) Garcia* told them the purpose of their mission, as Garcia believed that soldiers do a better job if they understand the reasons. Unlike the older officers, who generally don't trust the Indian recruits who comprise the bulk of the Ecuadorian army, Garcia was considered very politically "modern."

"Our beloved padre is coming home from the hospital today, and the men inside from the government museum are taking his collection into protective custody. They didn't expect him to survive the pneumonia and the prostate operation, not at his age, and he is going to be mad as hell. He is known for his quick temper—he's Italian. The point is, keep them separated and don't hurt the archaeologists either. Don't make a move without my orders. Be gentle but firm, and remember, the people in this town love him and think he is a saint."

Again, "Sí, jefe."

They tapped on the church door and were let in. The archaeologists, Olaf Holm and Reinoso Hermidia, approached Lieutenant Garcia. They looked nervous. "Lieutenant, this is serious business. The government has purchased this entire collection of artifacts from the church, and no one bothered to tell the priest. My boss, Señor Crespo, and Father Lova were sure he wouldn't survive the hospital. Now a doctor just called from the hospital that the priest, he's coming," said one of the archaeologists.

Garcia, a little annoyed, thought he knew the answer already and just wanted to needle the *scientificos*. "Did you buy the stuff directly from the priest, from Father Crespi himself?"

The archaeologist narrowed his eyes as Garcia's question had the desired effect, and the scientifico became annoyed. "No, the rector of

*Not his real name.

this church is Pedro Lova, Father Crespi's superior, and all the members of the Salesian order have taken vows of poverty, chastity, and above all, obedience. Crespi is no exception." Lieutenant Garcia said with emphasis, "*Father* Crespi."

The argument was getting heated and the archaeologist thought he had better pull in his horns. "Okay, *Father* Crespi is no exception to the rules. We have paid the church 113,000,000 sucres [almost $433,000] and this "stuff," as you put it, now belongs to the government, and when we are through evaluating and packing, it will go to the museum here in Cuenca for all the public to enjoy. That is that!"

"*Permítame* (Allow me), Señor, I was baptized by the good father, and I know him well. He is going to be furious, simply furious when he sees what you are doing."

"That is why the treasure, I mean the collection, is now under the protection of the army, and that is why you are here, lieutenant."

Suddenly the courtyard door banged open with a loud crash and the dreaded Italian whirlwind came roaring in. Cuenca is a small town and Padre Crespi had many devoted friends who had told him his life's work was being looted, and he was furious. They had tried to hold him at the hospital.

"You can't leave unless the doctor approves," they said. He roared back, "I'll leave when I please. Get me an ambulance or I'll walk." The staff rushed to get an ambulance.

At the church his walk was unsteady, and he was tottering and weak, but his fire was up. He saw the dozen workers manhandling his precious artifacts and let out a howl of rage. "What are you doing with my things?"

His superior, Pedro Lova, got between the outraged old man and the archaeologists and held his hands up to keep the combatants apart. Crespi was yelling loudly, "Get your hands off, get your hands off!" and his face had turned red. "Get your hands off my things. Those are mine." The ambulance driver put a firm but affectionate restraining hand on Crespi's arm and whispered, "Padrecito (little father), please get back on the gurney, you shouldn't even be out of the hospital. *Please.*" Then, with surprising speed for a ninety-year-old man, the enraged Crespi made an end run around his superior and yanked an extremely rare, ancient ceramic jar from the hands of a worker, all the while continuing to yell, "Get your hands off my stuff."

Finally recovering from the shock of Crespi's explosive presence, the archaeologist looked at the lieutenant and nodded. The nod was understood, and Garcia nodded in turn to his soldiers. They got between the workers and Crespi, ported their rifles chest high, and slowly shoved him away. They gently but firmly edged him toward his tiny bedroom on the edge of the courtyard.

The ambulance worker eased him onto the hard, wooden, newspaper-covered bed and gently put the worn blanket over him. He was breathing shallowly, and it was obvious the bronchopneumonia wasn't finished with him; then, exhausted, he sank into a troubled sleep. As he slept, the workers kept at it, lowering giant stone statues from upper balconies on ropes. The massive stone pieces were quickly loaded on trucks and hauled away.

The work began of sorting the nearly ten thousand artifacts the museum people had decided to take. It was one of the best hauls the museum had ever made, for had they bought it on the open market, it would have cost hundreds of times what they paid—a piddling forty-three dollars average per item. The church got horribly shortchanged, for on the open market or at auction, Crespi's collection would have brought in millions of dollars. Was the rector of the church, Father Pedro Lova, really that dense? The money ostensibly was to complete construction of a new school and continue Father Crespi's wonderful lunch program, so the kids, too, were shortchanged.

Now, where's the gold? Wayne May, publisher of *Ancient American* magazine, clearly remembers seeing photos of the disputed gold shown to him by Ecuador's newly installed director of archaeology. The pictures were taken by the archaeologist in the government museum in Cuenca, and the place at which he displayed the photos was a maverick conference, "Unsolved Mysteries," held in Vienna, Austria, in 2001 by Klaes Dona at the Vienna Arts Center. The director brought the photos of Crespi's treasures to share with the conference. The photos of the Cuenca museum's vault, with the steel door open, show the Crespi gold artifacts piled high and jammed to the ceiling. Wayne May remembers that there were many large items of gold. And they deliberately ignored the gold, so rumor had it, and anything that smacked of Crespi's crazy theories. Yet here were the gold artifacts that had been taken to the museum. The people who truly worried the established archaeologists were the younger Ecuadorian archaeologists who believe in the diffusion of culture; who believe that our ancestors, such as Vasco de Gama and Francis Drake, navigated the oceans and could sail completely around the world. Look at the people of Nigeria, who told early white explorers in Africa, "We used to paddle across the pond regularly to trade with the little brown people." The pond, of course, was the Atlantic Ocean.

In the magnificent Museo Nacional de Antropología in Mexico City, I once saw a photo of a Mayan wall mural from the Yucatan. It clearly showed black warriors selling bound white men to the brown Mayans, which shouldn't surprise us. The Midwestern Epigraphic Society has in its possession carved boulders from the Midwestern United States showing handsome and dignified black men and women who pre-date Christopher Columbus. As reported by *Midwestern Epigraphic Journal* and *Ancient American,* the boulders were excavated in the American Midwest by keen, reputable investigators who published their findings, which were subsequently ignored by the official archaeologists. After all, one said, "These people are just pot hunters and arrowhead collectors; they lack discipline, and they are uncredentialed." Little did he know that Barry Fell, Warren Cook, and the dozens of other experts are quite well credentialed. Just not accepted because of their nonconforming theories. What did the scientificos get when it was all over and the dust had settled? The museum counted their loot: more than ten thousand magnificent items. Seven thousand were pieces of fine, rare pottery representing all known ages of Ecuadorian culture (other than the earliest, the Valdivian period) that was so beautiful and valuable that it would be the envy of other museum curators. Then there were more than twelve hundred beautiful oil paintings, which the priest said were European Old Masters. Father Crespi claimed the paintings had been sent to him from Italy and France to avoid confiscation by the Fascists (National Socialists under Mussolini), and later by the Nazis (National Socialists under Hitler). He said that some of the oldest families in Italy, many of whom had relatives in the Salesian order, sent the paintings and other artwork to him for safekeeping.

Crespi was also legitimately dealing in antiquities from the early 1920s to the 1950s, before the government clamped the lid on exports. Ecuadorian customs agents confiscated a large batch of superb colonial paintings by local artists as the priest was trying to ship them to Europe for a sale. They are now in the museum.

What amazed the respected government agents, Olaf Holm and Reinoso Hermidia, was Crespi's sharp eye for beauty; they changed their opinion of him when they realized that he was a very discerning collector. Then why did he have a reputation for occasionally buying junk, like the decorated Ford clutch plate in fig. 3.21 or clumsily incised olive oil cans? His answer was, "They're hungry and very poor. This allows them a little dignity."

When people heard through the grapevine that the church was giving away Crespi's treasure, they showed up in droves. Two former pupils of Crespi who taught at a Peruvian-Ecuadorian border town showed up with a borrowed truck and, according to a church caretaker who witnessed with dismay, the two teachers took at least a full truckload of giant artifacts. Then there was the mysterious owner of the furniture factory, Atresanias Practicas, who took a liking to the artifacts and was allowed full, unsupervised access to Crespi's treasure. A massive collection of large square stones incised with a linear alphabet were part of his acquisition. The stones were later set in cement in the floor of his factory, where they can at least be studied, but regretfully, out of context. He is said to be the wealthiest man in Ecuador. And many loads of massive giant statues, at least forty of them, were supposedly taken to the secret military base of Cayambe, close to Cuenca, where they allegedly were set up as military trail markers.

The trucks continued loading for days, and where most of the collection went is a mystery. It was chaos, choking dust, and confusion, as the archaeologists Holm and Hermidia sat with damp handkerchiefs over their noses behind locked doors, feverishly trying to complete the massive project. Many of the workers and scientists still complain of serious, persistent breathing problems, reports anthropologist Warren Cook.

When Cook was there with photographer Warren Dexter, they had to literally beg Pedro Lova, the father superior, for permission to spend just a brief few minutes on the fourth floor where everything the two archaeologists hadn't chosen was piled helter skelter, and Cook picked from the dust a priceless gold child's tiara with a fairly substantial emerald that had been carelessly dropped on the floor amid the jumble. But the real enigma in this golden treasure was the images, for repoussé in the gold were pictures of genetically malformed "mixtures," half-human and half-animal, pathetically staring out at us over the centuries. Was this the evidence of ancient folklore? Or was this the perverted science of Atlantis?

There were also heavy golden helmets, one with what resembles a cartoon portrait of King Comus, the pre-Christian European king of the Mardi Gras. Other lighter crowns were obviously for ceremonial use with the gold armor, and some of Crespi's prized bronze plaques were lying about. During the very short time the men had available, they searched for another piece, a plate of gold showing a thirteen-step pyramid shown in plate 5, which Barry Fell told me was Paphian script from the Isle of Cyprus (although another linguist claims it is proto-Phoenician). They didn't find it. Was all the yellow stuff gold? Logic tells us that gold was common in the conquistadors' day. Atahualpa, the captured Inca, after having his shamans sacrifice five little boys on the altar because he had caught cold and wanted a quick cure, turned to the real problem at hand. He offered a room full of gold—twenty-two feet by seventeen feet by nine feet—3,366 square feet of golden objects and two equal-sized rooms full of silver if the Spaniards would free him. They assured him with solemn promises, "Yes, we'll free you when the gold is delivered." When the Spaniards took possession of the gold-filled room, and Pizarro, the boss, was conveniently away, Atahualpa was strangled. This was 1533. The indigenous peoples learned never to take the word of a conquistador, and if you were an Indian mother, never send your sons to Atahualpa—that is, if he had a cold.

But the story shows that there was plenty of gold in Ecuador, and when the Indian leaders realized what had been done to Atahualpa, they rushed to collect the rest of their gold relics and hide them. They hid an estimated ten to fifteen times the ransom payment. One small Spanish patrol reported pursuing a llama and cargo train and seeing a one-hundred-foot-long heavy golden chain, with each carrier handling one heavy link. In any event, the chain and the rest of the gold stripped from temple walls and other sacred places simply disappeared. So why dispute that the heavy, uncorroded, bright yellow stuff on display in 1978 was gold?

Difficult to miss among the padre's treasures would have been the golden, seven-foot tall, Egyptian-style mummy cases; however the two Warrens didn't see them in the jumbled attic. The mummy cases were similar to some in the collection of Israeli archaeologist and foreign minister Moshe Dayan, who had six of these sarcophagi in his personal collection. But none were of hammered gold like these. Perhaps they are still there somewhere, hidden under piles of debris. Perhaps they are in the museum's vault. Perhaps, as rumored in Cuenca, some of them decorate a rich man's fortresslike home.

One rumor says that some of the gold was shipped to the Vatican, but do we pay attention to rumors? Father Flores-Haro told Cook that official word came from the Vatican ordering that what was left of the treasure be kept out of the public sight. Again, *cui bono?*

The archaeologist who showed publisher Wayne May the photos of gold in the vault mysteriously dropped from sight, and May simply hasn't yet located him.

6

FAREWELL, MY FRIEND

TO BACKTRACK FOR JUST A MINUTE, Father Crespi's superior, Pedro Lova, had called the Central Bank in Quito and set in motion a hidden agenda, an event that had been on the back burner for many years—to crush Crespi's imaginative nonsense about Mediterranean visitors colonizing Ecuador. His odd theories were an embarrassment to the church, Pedro Lova told me on one visit to Cuenca. The plan was simple: use two reliable archaeologists with excellent establishment reputations and separate all the "good" stuff, giving it official approval, while the "junk," which was anything the crazy old Italian was fond of, was to be ignored, hidden away, or buried. As one archaeologist noted, most of what Crespi believed in—the huge rolls of gold and aluminum, the gold zodiac plate, the gold pyramid plate with Paphian-Cypriot linear writing, and the rest of the "fake" artifacts—was simply to be ignored and tossed aside. Señor Crespo, the chief in Quito's Central Bank museum, was quite sure that his loyal archaeologists would separate the junk and give the government museum only "genuine" artifacts. Crespo was absolutely certain his experts couldn't be fooled. In 1980, Crespo told Dexter and Cook that an acquaintance of his, the editor of *Revista Anthropologico,* had told him, "As for that sheet metal, which he calls wall covering, it is only fit to be melted down; while the rest of it is pure nonsense made by local artisans to fool a gullible old priest."

I wanted to pay my respects to that gullible old priest and see Carlo Crespi before he passed on, so I took a flight to Quito and jumped on an Andes mountain bus up over the clouds to Cuenca for my last visit. A battered old taxi dropped me at the front door of the church, and there in the courtyard stood Father Crespi surrounded by a group of loving admirers. *"Dame un bendicion,"* they were saying. (Give me a blessing.) In the group surrounding him were beggars in ragged clothing alongside a few obviously prosperous middle-class people. I saw him reach into his pocket and pull out a handful of coins for the poor children clustered around him. He saw me and walked quickly away from his admirers to his tiny room, just off the courtyard. He ducked in and came out with a great smile on his face, carrying a favorite object. It was my favorite too, a heavy, cast-bronze plaque of an exotic lady dressed in a royal head-dress. I think of her as an Atlantean princess, but her face, especially her almond eyes, reminds me of a male Etruscan statue. "The Apollo of Veii from the sixth century BCE, Reechard," he exulted triumphantly. "They didn't get it all." Then he reached into his tiny bedroom and pulled four more bronze plaques from under the newspaper-padded bed. There was the "Goliath" plaque, complete with a dent in his forehead from David's sling stone, and to give you an idea of Goliath's size, he is holding a man's severed head on a pole; the head is half the size of the giant's. Then there was the "David" plaque, with David holding a severed giant's head that is twice as big as David's. Then he pulled out a plaque of an Assyrian sacred five-legged bull, and next was an Assyrian Nisroch figure.

Crespi was tired; he was nearly ninety and had just gotten out of the hospital. He had also endured the roaring shock of the confiscation of his precious artifacts—his life's work. We talked for a while and then he was tired and lay down. Sadly, after a warm visit I said good-bye and left; there was nothing more I could do.

DINNER
CONVERSATION

A Boiled Fish Surprise

THE SUN HAD JUST VANISHED toward Miami, and I was enjoying a bowl of delicious Bahamian fish soup laced with just the right amount of chili peppers in a restaurant on South Bimini, when my stepson Mike came in with another man. My stepson, democratically friendly and outgoing, apparently had a new friend. They didn't see me at first, so I watched from the shadows as they ordered grilled grouper and a couple of Beck's beers.

Mike's buddy looked like a typical Latino thug. He was stocky and about five foot eight, with thick black hair combed straight back, Indian style. His skin was a distinct copper color, but his eyes were deep, focused green, reflecting Spanish genes. He wore heavy gold bracelets on his arms and a double gold chain around his thick neck. His fingers were covered with rings, and the large sparkling stones in the rings were, without a doubt, real diamonds. He looked like the typical get-it-quick-and-lose-it-quicker smuggler in the frontline war to coke up America. When the manager turned up the overhead lights, Mike and his newfound buddy saw me and began an animated conversation while glancing at me. Then Mike motioned me over to his table for one of the best dinner conversations I've ever had.

"Richard, this is Carlos. He has something wild to tell you. He thinks you'll be interested," Mike began. I sat down, just a little wary. Mike continued, "I've been telling Carlos about your discoveries of the high-tech inventions of Atlantis, and your theory of the people the Spanish call 'ignorant Indians,' who were anything but ignorant, has him all enthused. I told him of the marble building we saw here in the Bahamas under only twenty-two feet of water and cleaned off with our sand duster. And I told him about your photographs of the Crespi Collection. That's when he got excited."

Carlos guzzled another beer and Mike translated. "*Soy Colombiano* (I'm Colombian). One night last year I was drinking in a bar in Cali, Colombia, and I struck up a conversation with a gringo. We hit it off and ended up going to another club—a very exclusive club. Very expensive. Really good-looking women. Some of them were even from Russia. The man's name was Estan. He had lots of money. During the course of the night we both got very sloshed, and we went on drinking nonstop for two days. I had a great time with Estan.

"Estan told me he had been on an expedition to the jungles of Ecuador where he'd located the caves of Carlos Crespi, the fabulous treasure trove of the Shuara headhunter people. There were eight American scientists on the trip and a handful of support people. Estan never told me their names, but he said they found loads of treasure, lots of gold, gold armor, gold wall coverings like wallpaper but thicker; and all kinds of ancient artifacts, such as heavy copper objects, and machinery with wheels and gears. Estan said he knew it was machinery but didn't know what it was for, perhaps for grinding grain. The thing about the machinery was the peculiar red color of the metal. There was a metallurgist with the team, and he got very excited and began testing metals. First he tested the red-colored metal for hardness. He let out a cry that it was as hard as steel. Then he picked up a large square of sheet metal, and it tested as aluminum. But best of all was a square of iron he tapped with a hammer. It didn't ring—he hit it very hard, and it just thudded. I'm not technically inclined, but even I could see that a man could make a lot of money with an invention like that. Then a lady scientist found a giant throne with a lot of other furniture. It was big enough for a giant and decorated with gemstones, but the metal looked like tin, so she gave it a shove. She was startled when it tilted over with the tiniest push, almost as if it didn't weigh anything. She lifted it up and swung it over her head with just one hand. A weightless throne. Talk about the money you could make with that. Then she lost her cool and laughed hysterically. I think that Estan had found Father Crespi's secret tunnels, at least that's what he told me. I had never heard of Crespi before this. Estan said he had been searching for Crespi's tunnels for years. Finally, with some real money put up by some big shot—he didn't tell me who—Estan had hit the big time."

Carlos' story thrilled me. It put missing pieces of the archaeological puzzle in place.

Are there other groups equally determined to keep us from discovering the past? The aristocrats who control our governments from behind the scenes, or the greedy who want discoveries from the technological past to remain buried until they have figured out a way to profit from it? There are probably other reasons, such as the possibility of unearthing now unknown combat technologies.

One afternoon, years after this South Bimini boiled fish surprise, I was in El Salvador having lunch with a group of farmers in the town of Ahuachapan when a farmer offered to sell me something his plow had uncovered. It was a small, torpedo-shaped ceramic object, about six inches long. It contained a cockpit with two male figures in it, facing forward. The torpedo had a low windshield, sort of like a motorcycle. The craft had no roof, no propeller or nacelles for engines, but it did have an aileron with a vane on the rear. Was it a model of an antigravity craft? Knowing the secret of antigravity craft would make any modern armed forces commander drool. So long, that is, as the enemy didn't know the secret.

Is it possible that some of the super wealthy and powerful are mining our archaeological past for private motives and distorting our history in the bargain?

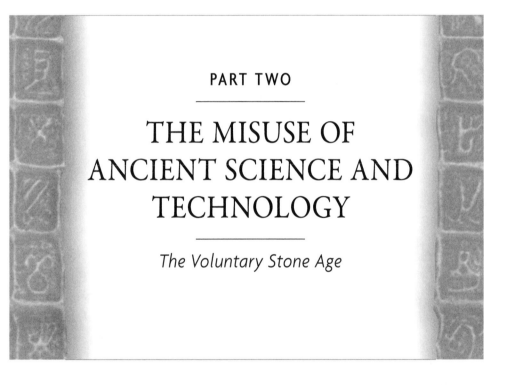

PART TWO

THE MISUSE OF ANCIENT SCIENCE AND TECHNOLOGY

The Voluntary Stone Age

THE MYSTERIOUS
DISAPPEARANCE OF
PERCY FAWCETT

THE INDIAN SHAMAN applied a secret salve and a bloated maggot poked out of the opening in explorer Percy Fawcett's wiry forearm and emerged into the light. When it got above the skin, the shaman pinched it between his thumb and forefinger, and it popped out of its bloody hole. The explorer treated the open wound with iodine, and then he did something that was unusual for him—he smiled.

Fawcett was a lieutenant colonel in the British army, stationed along the uncharted border between Bolivia and Brazil. His mission: map the border for the governments of Paraguay, Bolivia, Peru, Brazil, and, of course, imperial England. The time: the early part of 1912. The colonel spent years—starting in 1906—mapping the unknown areas, funded in part by the British Royal Geographical Society, and he gave them their money's worth. He did a splendid job of mapping the national borders while also learning how to survive in the jungle. A tough, disciplined man, even he found the Brazilian-Bolivian rain forest a frightful place. He and his team of explorers slept under mosquito nets for protection from the many flying and creepy crawlies of the night, but if they so much as let a body part brush against the netting, lurking creatures would take advantage. *The Lost City of Z*, a nonfiction account by David Grann, recounts the aforementioned maggot story, and it is a thrilling read. Fawcett also referred to the maggots in his diary.

The jungle is loaded with nasties. One of the perils is vampire bats—bloodsuckers with razor sharp incisors that slice a painless cut over the veins of the victim, then fan their wings very slowly to keep the sleeping victim cool while they lap his blood; their saliva contains an anesthetic, so the poor victim doesn't feel the wound. The tiny ihenni fly, or no-see-ums, are small enough to pass through the mesh of the mosquito net and cause many a lost night's sleep. Then there is fungus; it proliferates in the damp and can rot the skin or discolor it for life. There are venomous spiders, ticks, fleas, lice, chiggers, ants, cannibal piranha fish, and dozens of biting things, including the deadly Fer de Lance snake; but what the natives fear most is the giant anaconda snake, not poisonous but large and powerful enough to crush a full-grown person with ease and swallow the victim whole. During one expedition into the Mato Grosso section of Brazil, Grann reports that Fawcett killed an anaconda that was a foot wide and sixty-two feet in length.

In addition to these mobile creatures, the trees often protect themselves with spines and stickers, so one must be careful, no matter how tired, never to lean against anything. And the thick tree canopy shuts out direct sunlight, bathing the jungle with a psychologically depressing, sickly gray-green cast.

But the most tormenting factor is the humidity, which is near total saturation. Imagine living, walking, cooking, eating, and trying to sleep in a continual steam bath so intense that the natives brave the hazards and go naked. It is also easier to pick crawling insects off bare skin than search through a layer of clothing.

During the years he spent surveying, Fawcett talked with hundreds of people who knew the jungle: rubber tappers, soldiers, timber cutters, priests, and local natives. He gradually pieced together a consistent story of lost cities, and his corroborating details convinced Fawcett that there had been a great civilization in the Mato Grosso in the Brazilian Amazon. One document dated 1753 in a museum in Sao Paulo, Brazil, told of an ancient hidden abandoned city in the Serra do Roncador near the Rio Xingu, a tributary of the Amazon. He found many other references to cities that glowed a soft moonlit blue when the sun went down.

As Fawett recounts in his diary, these cities were peopled with a race of ferocious fighting Indians with white skin, golden blonde, red, or auburn hair, and delicate hands and feet. Fawcett lived with one tribe called the Tapuyas, which was "as fair as the average Englishman," quotes Fawcett in his diary. Fawcett said the Tapuyas were excellent jade carvers and jewelry makers who told of vast treasures, including gold-covered abandoned temples. More sobering, his diary foretold, he heard the chances of coming out alive were slim. Reminding him of this truth was a documented account of a 1650 expedition of fourteen hundred heavily armed soldiers searching the rain forest for the lost city of Manoa who disappeared into the jungle and were never heard from again.

Jesuit missionary priests in the 1700s reported many lost cities in the Mato Grosso, but were scoffed at by geographical experts, who insisted the jungle couldn't support a large enough population to people a giant city. The soil is too poor and the topsoil washes away during the ferocious, everlasting torrential rains.

Fawcett's senior officers admonished, "You are letting your head swell with drunken campfire stories made up by racial inferiors. Stick to surveying, Colonel, you're good at that." His honor offended, Fawcett quit the army and lectured with the Royal Geographical Society, raising money for a civilian expedition to find Manoa, the lost city of gold.

While staying in Sri Lanka, his brother filled him in on Buddhism, The Masters, and Helena Blavatsky. He was fascinated by Blavatsky's true story of being shot while fighting for Garibaldi's revolution to unify Italy. Hit by a sixty-caliber bullet, she loudly threatened battlefield surgeons with death if they dared try to amputate her bullet-shattered leg. She recovered by force of will and walked again, but with a limp. She was Percy's kind of person.

Blavatsky had written of her efforts to find a lost city when she was previously exploring South America, and this convinced Fawcett that the legends and stories were true and even more incredible than he'd imagined, and that these cities had been colonies of Atlantis. If Blavatsky's *The Secret Doctrine* was indeed accurate in mentioning Atlantis, then finding an ancient technological civilization abandoned in antiquity would be confirmation of her claims. No doubt Fawcett had also read Besant's previously mentioned book, *Man, Whence, How, and Whither*, which told of Atlantean colonies in Peru.

Finding a colony of Atlantis would also be a dramatic first step toward proving the existence of the "Brotherhood of Saints," believed by Besant and Blavatsky to be the secret driving force behind productive change in our world. Typical of the scorn heaped on Fawcett's plans was the sentiment of one bewhiskered, "fat and extremely wealthy British graybeard: Balderdash. Fawcett, inspired by Blavatsky and Besant together, a lunatic asylum in triplicate. I wouldn't give him a penny."

Experience had taught Fawcett that a large team was expensive, clumsy, and dangerous—look at the fourteen hundred soldiers who had disappeared. His small team would include only himself, his son Jack, and Jack's best friend, Raleigh Rimmel, a newspaper photographer.

In 1925, Fawcett and his party took a steamer to the port of Manaus, two thousand miles up the Amazon from the Atlantic Ocean, then transferred to a smaller boat for the forbidding trip deep into the rain forest. Then they disappeared forever.

Many expeditions have searched unsuccessfully for the missing explorers. The last was in 1996 when a well-financed and equipped party from Germany searching for Fawcett was captured by a hostile tribe and relieved of all their goods, outboard motors, rifles, and the rest. The rain forest is still dangerous, and the German leader was fortunate he got out with his life.

However, recent aerial surveys followed by ground exploration of the Mato Grosso have shown a series of great rectangles, artfully laid out. When a helicopter team landed on one of the locations, they found good black earth fertilized with human waste and charcoal, and very cultivable soil, capable of supporting a great population.

It is unclear whether Fawcett ever found what he sought. Before his last departure he left a note for his wife, saying, "You need have no fear of failure." She never heard from him again.

LEGENDS OF ATLANTIS

ATLANTIS WAS REPUTED to have been a large island in the Atlantic Ocean stretching from the Azores islands off the coast of Portugal all the way west to the present-day Bahamas. It had a powerful civilization and controlled most of the world through its colonies. The island was peopled by the red race, and if you want to know what they looked like, think of the Native American Chief Joseph, a noble leader of the Native Americans in the American West in the 1800s.

The Greek philosopher Plato describes an Atlantic island-continent in his *Critias* (360 BCE) and other dialogues. On the far side of this island lay another continent with large herds of great beasts. This is a possible reference to the bison.

Just before imperial Atlantis's final collapse, it sent a giant-sized army to subdue the remainder of our globe. Plato's *Critias* dialogue tells the story of heroic Greeks who defeated an Atlantean grand army of a million men (see below and also see appendix 1). The Athenian army was later destroyed by cataclysmic flooding when earthquakes and a tidal wave smashed apart the Gibraltar land bridge that connected Africa with Europe, allowing in the waters of the Atlantic Ocean, which filled the Mediterranean valley with roaring waves and drowned the

Hellenes, ancient Greece. According to Plato, the landmass of present-day Greece and the Greek islands are all that remains of a much larger Greek nation. The grand size of that Greek nation would account for an Athenian navy massive enough to defeat an Atlantean million-man invasion.

The story of Solon, one of the seven revered lawgivers of ancient Greece, was passed down to Plato by an Egyptian priest-historian from the city of Sais in Egypt.

Psonchis: Solon, you remember only one deluge, whereas there were many deluges before that. . . . Many great and wonderful deeds are recorded of your state in our histories, but one of these exceeds all the rest in greatness and valor, for this histories tell of a mighty power, which was aggressing wantonly against the whole of Europe and Asia, and to which your city put an end. This power had landed on the Atlantic coast, for in those days the Atlantic was navigable from an island situated to the west of the straits, which you call the Pillars of Hercules. The island was larger than Libya and Asia put together, and from it could be reached other islands. And from the islands you might pass through to the opposite continent, which surrounded the true ocean, for this sea, which is within the columns of Hercules, is only a harbor having a narrow entrance, but that other is a real sea and the surrounding land may be most truly called a continent. Now the island was called Atlantis and was the heart of a great and wonderful empire, which had rule over the whole island and several others, as well as over parts of the continent; and besides these they subjected parts of Libya [Africa] as far as Egypt, and of Europe as far as Tyrrhenia [Switzerland]. The vast power thus gathered into one endeavored to subdue at one blow our country and yours, and the whole of the land. Having undergone the very extremity of danger, she defeated and triumphed over the invaders and preserved from slavery those who were not yet subjected, and freely liberated all the others who dwelt within the limits of Heracles. And then, Solon, your country shone forth in the excellence of her virtue and strength among all mankind, for she was the first in courage and military skill, and was the leader of the Hellenic allies. And when the rest fell off from her, being compelled to stand alone after having undergone the very extremity of danger, she defeated and triumphed over the invaders and preserved from slavery those who were not yet subjected, and freely liberated all others who dwelt within the limits of Heracles. But afterward there occurred violent earthquakes and floods, and in a single day and night of rain, all your warlike men, in a body, sank into the earth, and the island of Atlantis in like manner disappeared beneath the sea.

Later in the dialogue, Psonchis describes the Atlantean race:

For many generations, as long as the divine nature lasted in them, they were obedient to the laws and well affectioned toward the God who was their kinsman, for they possessed true and in every way great spirits, practicing gentleness and wisdom in the various changes of life, in their intercourse with one another.

They despised everything but virtue, not caring for their present state of life and thinking lightly on the possession of gold and other property, which seemed only a burden to them. Neither were they intoxicated by luxury, nor did wealth deprive them of their self-control, but they were sober and saw clearly that all these goods are increased by virtuous friendship with one another, and that by excessive zeal for them and honor of them, the good of them is lost and friendship perishes with them. By such reflections and by the continuance in them of a divine nature, all that we have described waxed and increased in them and became diluted too often and with too much of the mortal admixture, and human nature got the upper hand. They being unable to bear their fortune became unseemly and to him who had eye to see they began to appear base, and had lost the fairest of their previous gifts; but to those who had no eye to see true happiness, they still appeared glorious and blessed at the very time when they were filled with unrighteous avarice and power.

The Greek philosopher Aristotle, whose theory that Earth was the center of our universe was accepted until challenged by the astronomer Copernicus in the sixteenth century, said something like, "Phooey on Plato's Atlantis." He didn't believe in it, and he irritably dismissed Plato. After all, Aristotle was the darling of the church, and if you believe Plato was right, you have to believe that we are sons and daughters of the gods, the very descendants of extraterrestrials.

Researchers say that the historian Herodotus visited Egypt around 500 BCE and reported that Egyptian priests dated their written history back to 113 centuries before his arrival, or 11,300 years ago. He wrote that he had seen 341 statues of high priests who had succeeded one another during that time period, indicating an average reign of thirty-three years apiece. The high priests told of an ancient island paradise situated far west of the Columns of Heracles: Atlantis. And Krantor, one of Plato's pupils, claimed to have seen in Egypt a column or stele that verified Solon's story of Atlantis. "I have seen the evidence," he claimed, "and it is preserved by the Egyptian priests."

Manetho the Mendesian in 250 BCE wrote, "The Egyptians obtained their hieroglyphic writing from a drowned continent."

In the first century BCE Diodorus Siculus wrote: ". . . for there lies out in the deep, off Libya, an island of considerable size." And, "The kingdom of Atlantoi was divided among the sons of Uranus." And, "The Phoenicians got their alphabet from the island of Atlantis."*

There are many hundreds of references to the drowned continent, but one stands out. The story called the *Oera Linda Boek,* which some brave European scholars believe is the oldest surviving Gothic document in Europe. This astonishing text came to light in the mid-1800s

---

*From *The Library of History.*

in Holland. The prominent Over de Linden family guarded the *Oera Linda Boek* as a family treasure and kept it hidden. Then Cornelius Over de Linden, head of the family and respected director of the Royal Netherlands Shipyards, mentioned the *Oera Linda Boek* to a leading Dutch scholar, Dr. E. Verwijs. Cornelius said he couldn't read the document and was curious about its contents. Verwijs organized a study group, which began an examination. They prepared a Dutch text in 1872, and an English translation was published in 1876. After the initial predictably angry denunciations, various credentialed authorities began to support the document's authenticity. Dr. J. R. Vitringa, one of the text's earlier critics, apologized for his first reaction and admitted that further study had led him to a firm belief in the document's authenticity.

Another manuscript preserved by the Over De Linden family is a letter written by their ancestor Hiddo, who recopied the *Oera Linda Boek* in 1256 CE to his son Okke:

> Okke, my son, you must keep these books with body and soul. In them is the history of our people. Last year I saved them from the flood at the time when I saved your mother and you. They got wet and began to perish. To preserve, I have copied them on foreign paper. When you inherit them you must promise to copy them and so must your children. That way they will never be lost.

The *Oera Linda Boek* describes an ancient period of great natural upheavals.

> Before the bad flood came, our land was the most beautiful in the world. The sun rose higher in those days and there was seldom any frost. The trees and shrubs produced fruits that we no longer know. They have been lost. Our fields produced oats, barley, and rye, and a golden wheat, which could be dried in the sun. Some baked their wheat with the sun. The years were never counted because one

year was as happy as those that had passed. On one side we were hemmed in by Twiskland, by which Finda's people dared not come. Twiskland had dense forests and many wild and dangerous animals. . . . Opposite to us was West Britanja, which we called Westland. There were tin mines there, and our sailors and merchants had many factories and posts in Lydia, where the people are black.

During the whole summer the sun was hidden behind the clouds as though it would never shine again upon our world. There was a perpetual calm. A damp mist hung like a wet cloth over the homes and marshes. The air was heavy and still. People became sad. In the midst of this stillness, the earth began to tremble as if she were undergoing convulsions. Mountains vomited fire and flames. Some countries sank into the earth while others rose out of the valleys and plains.

. . . Atland, the motherland to the west, beyond Britanja, vanished, and the wild water rose so high over the hills and valleys that everything was buried beneath the sea. Many people were swallowed up by the earth.

Others who escaped death by fire were lost in the high waves. It was not only in Finda's land that the earth belched fire, but also in Twiskland. Big forests were burnt one after the other. When the wind blew from that place our land was covered with ashes. Rivers changed their courses. At their mouths new islands were formed out of sand and drift.

For three years this never stopped, but at last it ceased. The forests again became visible to us. Many countries were sunk beneath the waters. In other places, new land rose up out of the sea. The woods were destroyed through half of Twiskland. Many of Finda's people came and settled in these barren lands. Our people who had fled to Twiskland were exterminated or enslaved. Our watchfulness increased and we learned that union is strength.

The document maintains that after a century of vicious anarchy, rule by law was eventually, painfully restored and international trade began again. Since the *Oera Linda Boek* is so old and has been copied so many times, there is a distinct possibility that the writers are mixing their cataclysms. The phrase, "the mist hung over the land" and reference to the terrible upheavals may have been confused between the sinking of Atlantis and the subsequent Fimbul winter. No one really knows.

We can, however, make educated guesses, which is what the remainder of this book is about; I hope it resonates with you.

THE
PANECILLO LASER

A PREHISTORIC LASER, really, sitting on top of the largest human-made mound on earth, and the mound is designed and shaped like a giant sperm cell. On perhaps one of the largest human engineered structures on earth sits the visible remains of what may have been one of the world's first laser transmission stations. The giant curved mound is called El Panecillo, the breakfast bread roll (pan-a-see-yo).

Panecillo, which lies within the city limits of Quito, Ecuador, at 9,200 feet elevation, is so big it can be seen from nearly every neighborhood in Quito. It is overshadowed by a semi-circle of active volcanos, cloud wreathed and still quietly breathing an ominous hint of future eruptions. However, the people of Quito are so used to the volcanoes that they don't pay them any mind. After all, it was a long time ago that the last one went off. Who worries?

To prove Mother Nature's even-handedness, however, the volcanic ash quickly, as geologic time goes, erodes into a thick, black mineral-rich soil, turning Ecuador into one of the world's most lush gardens. I remember seeing a small boy carrying two giant cabbages grown from this rich soil. Threaded through their thick stems with homemade sisal rope handles; he staggered under his heavy load.

Quito, though nearly straddling the equator, has perhaps one of the most enjoyable climates in the world, that is, once you get accustomed to the altitude, with the four seasons repeating themselves daily, spring in the morning, summer at noon, fall in the afternoon, and then the chilly winter at night. Bring a warm sweater or a topcoat if you plan to visit.

Dressed stone, taken from ancient structures that once dotted Panecillo, are embedded in the foundations and walls of recently built mud and brick houses nestling placidly on this mound.

Hire a taxi to the top of Panecillo. Or take a local bus for a satisfying 35 cents American, but you'll have to share the bus with the local natives who often carry chickens and guinea pigs.

Now about the prehistoric laser: A teenage boy walking atop Panecillo, stepped into a soft spot on the mound, the dirt gave way, and he fell into a hole and broke his leg. He had, unfortunately for him, discovered a structure that had been buried so long, that even the Quiteno tribe, who lived there, a long time before the Incas, had no memory of it. When the local archaeologists uncovered it, they found a dome-shaped building made of a peculiar brick with a carefully crafted, circular opening in the roof. Extending from its lower portion was a tunnel made from granite, glued together with the ubiquitous metallic cement of Atlantis. The tunnel has a keystone, or Roman arch; very peculiar, because the natives of South America, including the Incas, used overlapping stone to make their arches, and as far as I know, this is the only ancient Roman arch in the Americas. The carefully fitted stonework on the exit tunnel shows that they could have built the building with granite, if they chose, or any other stone, so why did the builders use brick for the main structure. Cayce said it was firebrick. Why did the people who buried this structure chisel off the facing stones of the arch? What didn't they want us, in the future, to see? At the exit to the tunnel sits a piece of basalt rock, cut to fit over a curved channel, possibly a circulating drain, which, if you follow the curve, leads back into the building. The basalt column has been broken off, and radiating from it are a series of lines, set in the dirt floor, which might have been used to sight the device. This building is a true out of place artifact, an oopart. A pretty fair guess is that the ancient peoples had technology and deliberately abandoned it. Of course the machinery inside has been destroyed or hidden.

A clue to its construction was given in 1933, by clairvoyant Edgar Cayce (in reading #440-5, December 20, 1933), of a building that housed the Firestone of Atlantis. The Firestone was a ruby colored, faceted glass, probably a Fresnel lens, which was once used in modern lighthouses, which focused the sun's rays and, Cayce said, it was housed in a natural beehive-shaped dome built of firebrick Surrounding the beehive is a watertight stone moat that still holds rainwater. He said, "in the center of a building, which would be said to be lined with . . . non-conductive stone, something akin to asbestos with other non-conductors . . . the building above the fire-stone was oval, or a dome wherein there could be a portion for rolling back so that the concentration of energies that emanate from bodies that are on fire, (the sun) . . . so that which was impelled by the concentration of rays from the stone, which was centered in the middle of the power station, or powerhouse." Cayce's convoluted syntax suggests, to some linguists, a computer language. Regardless of where Cayce got his material for the "readings," he got his information in 1933, twenty-five years before the modern laser was activated. He also said the beam emitted by the firestone powered their aircraft by induction, and, also, all the machinery of Atlantis.

Also, he said, the beam was invisible to the eye, and when our first modern laser was activated, it emitted an intense ruby-colored, visible beam, but a short time later when a laser was pumped with sunlight, the rays were invisible. As bizarre as Edgar Cayce's readings seem to be, they were right on target.

Fig. 10.1. Sperm cell snout of Panecillo. Quito lies below.

Fig. 10.2. The sperm cell tail of Panecillo

Fig. 10.3. *La Olla* or The Oven. Strange building from prehistory recently uncovered on the top of Panecillo. This dome has no architectural counterparts in the entire world, except for the mysterious melted wall "Scottish Ovens" with circular openings in their tops.

Fig. 10.4. *La Olla*. Outside entrance of tunnel. Facing stones have been removed.

Fig. 10.5. *La Olla*. Blackened line of original landscaping seen to right of tunnel.

Fig. 10.6. *La Olla*. Circulating drain.

THE POWERFUL
WOODEN UFOS

THE PILOT OF THE Messerschmitt 109, the Germans' fastest and most maneuverable fighter plane at the beginning of World War II, let his plane go full throttle. The plane strained but still couldn't catch up with the mysterious British bomber, the Mosquito, which was pulling away from him at more than four hundred miles per hour. Amazingly, the British mystery plane was made almost entirely of wood. It would surprise both the pilots who flew it and the engineers who designed the Mosquito that lightweight laminated wood was mentioned in ancient Hindu history books as having been used in flying craft many thousands of years ago. The Hindu texts tell of ancient flying ships made of wood and other materials, called *vimanas*. One section of the massive hundred-thousand-verse Mahabharata introduces us to two technical specialists, master carpenters who were in charge of building flying craft in ancient India. The secret ingredient, which the British de Haviland engineers rediscovered, was lightweight laminated balsa wood from Ecuador. Laminated wood gave the bomber a low-radar profile, and it was extremely lightweight, with a phenomenally high strength-to-weight

92

ratio. Perhaps Hans Solo's fictional *Millennium Falcon* in *Star Wars* had a wooden superstructure as well; after all, it outran the imperial fighters. But let's get back to the Mosquito bomber. By accidentally rediscovering the ancient Hindu technology, or at least one of their secrets, Geoffrey de Haviland, the aircraft factory founder, helped confirm one small bit of ancient technology: that wood is good material for flying craft.

This brings us to John Searle, an English inventor who also rediscovered ancient Hindu technology by using wooden struts and plywood to build his IFOs (Identified Flying Objects), a story reported by both British television and newspapers. Searle had no problem getting his circular craft to fly; however, he didn't know how to bring them back home. He sent several off into the wild blue yonder, but none of them returned.

Searle did stumble onto one basic fact of antigravity: that "a spinning-centrifugal force field loses weight and can be induced to lift off with its centrifugally activated, zero-point propulsion." Strangely enough, the Hindu history books also refer to centrifugal force for propulsion.

On the other side of the Atlantic, a Canadian professor named Eric Laithwaite also uncovered the Hindu secret of propelling flying craft when he discovered that a spinning gyroscope loses weight; in other words, it gets lighter. Knowing this basic fact, a team of bright engineers could work out the math and probably wouldn't find it too difficult to come up with a workable flying craft. Laithwaite's heart was in the right place, and he didn't patent his discovery but left it free for the world. That might have been his critical error, as no banker could get a monopoly on his invention. Mysteriously, or perhaps not so mysteriously, Laithwaite's standing in the scientific community took a sudden nosedive. He was widely discredited, ran into a news blackout, and little has been heard from him since.

A German forestry expert, Viktor Schauberger, discovered something similar while observing trout swimming upstream to mate. The fish would spin as they jumped, allowing them to leap higher than seemed possible. Duplicating the trout's amazing leap, he spun water in a circular tube and discovered it would generate vast quantities of electricity, but would also lose weight and could be induced to "lift off" the surface. Germans scientists and engineers worked furiously on this invention and launched a few craft, and soon Allied pilots were turning in reports of circular flying craft moving at high speed and outmaneuvering our bombers and fighters. Puzzled, the Allied flyers called the mysterious spheres "foo fighters." Fortunately for the Allies, the war with Germany was almost over and Allied intelligence, hot on the trail of the collapsing Wermacht, rushed to the Skoda arms factory in Pilsen, Czechoslovakia, to pick up the scientific pieces of Schauberger's secret weapon and other equally fearsome war machinery. Allied intelligence officers were awestruck when they discovered that Adolf Hitler, when boasting of really ferocious weapons, really did have them. Hitler, to boost failing morale, had bragged to the German people of secret weapons in his arsenal, and German scientists were indeed working on frightening secret weapons.

The then prime minister of Great Britain, Winston Churchill, informed by his intelligence operatives, referred chillingly to Germany's "perverted science." The Germans had already flown their newest bomber to New York City, where the aircrew delightedly tuned into a jazz radio broadcast before turning back to Europe, and now rumors bounced wildly as the intelligence community excitedly whispered of a workable atomic bomb almost ready for its first deadly trip to Washington, D.C.

Fortunately, the Allies had reached the secret laboratories before the weapons could be mass-produced. Our agents scooped up the German scientists and their entire laboratories and scooted them across the Atlantic to their new home in the American Southwest. The German scientists, including Werner von Braun and some of his scientist colleagues, were made "an offer they couldn't refuse," and German scientists doggedly went to work for the new bosses, designing bigger and better rockets to carry bigger and better nuclear weapons. And in addition, they eagerly picked up on Schauberger's work.

The theory behind antigravity propulsion seems simple. Imagine a powerful energy envelope encapsulating every particle of matter—a powerful matrix. Surrounded by this pressurized envelope, all we have to do is punch a hole in the envelope to create a neutral center or zero point, keep the hole open, and the energy would pour into this—our dimension—under pressure, in much the same way that liquid under pressure squirts from a bung hole when a beer barrel is tapped.

An electric generator "cuts" magnetic lines of force and "leaks" electrons, which we call electricity. Think of an electric generator as a pump. It is not "generating" or creating electricity, but pumping it from one dimension into another.

What Laithwaite, Searle, the Germans, and the ancient Hindu scientists all discovered was how to centrifugally poke a hole in the pressurized energy envelope surrounding us, creating a neutral center or zero point that allowed the juice, quite simply, to flow into this dimension with all the pressure of the universe behind it. Fastened in a frame, this zero-point motor would automatically reject Earth's gravity and fly. It wasn't a question of how to get the craft to fly, but of mastering the art of how to steer it and how to bring it back. This discovery, when harnessed, is also a source of free energy, which would feed the world's energy appetite quite nicely. And it's free! Well, almost free, as there might be hidden factors involved. We'll have to wait until the world is politically ready.

12

THE MAHABHARATA

MURDER, NOBILITY, TREACHERY, betrayed love, personal combat between powerful men competing for fabulously beautiful women, magnificent great wealth, jealousy, intrigue, and global war, which the good guys won . . . The story begins on the banks of the sacred Indus River, settled by horsemen nomads from Asia, some say Mongolia. They called themselves Aryans, which means "noble" in Sanskrit, their language. They were white skinned, and they first made their appearance on the world stage many thousands of years ago. Mohenjo Daro, their nuclear-destroyed city, has been traced back to at least six thousand years ago by establishment archaeologists, though some investigators believe it is much, much older. We do know this about the Aryans: they had a special talent for science and technology. They also knew the secrets of prosperity, which were order, social stability, personal honesty, and a willingness to take risks: the same methods practiced by the early Romans until Rome rotted from its own prosperity and was overwhelmed by the less noble.

The Aryans and their science brought India to a high level of prosperity, and until the British invaded, India was the richest collection of small nations on earth. Diamonds, silk, spices, and other luxuries brought traders from all over the world. Columbus, after all, was searching for a direct route to the Indies when he bumped into the Americas.

The Mahabharata details an ancient war between the two empires of Aryan India and Aryan Atlantis fighting for control of the world. It is the best-loved book in India, as well as the oldest history. The Indian people love it so much that even today many professional storytellers memorize portions of it and go from village to village earning their living by giving recitations. Especially treasured is the section known as the "Bhagavad Gita" (The Song of God), the story of Krishna and Arjuna.

What interests us today are realistic, detailed stories of long ago, telling of sophisticated technology and science. Why is it that we in the "modern" world don't know about the technological information revealed in this ancient book? Our European languages have Sanskrit roots, or at the very least have borrowed heavily from the Hindus who spoke ancient Sanskrit. If our Hindu ancestors had antigravity aircraft, lasers, atomic weapons, radar, sophisticated city planning, beautiful irrigation systems, and all the other technological appurtenances of civilization, then what happened to them? Where is the evidence?

The Mahabharata, the ancient history of the Hindis, tells us that a Hindu king of the Ghurka peoples launched nuclear-tipped rockets at enemy cities, and the rockets exploded with the roar of ten thousand hurricanes. Elephants that were miles away were knocked off their feet, there was a flash like ten thousand suns, an umbrella-shaped cloud rose to the heavens, and all the other phenomena of an exploding nuclear bomb, including poisonous radioactive fallout appeared. The literal fallout from Ghurka's atomic attack on his enemies caused the king to feel sorrow for what he had done, and he ordered the iron thunderbolt rocket destroyed—the nuclear warheads ground into powder and cast into the river. His repentance was repeated many thousands of years later by the Indian king, Ashoka (256–237 BCE) who became a peaceful Buddhist and ordered all weapons of mass destruction buried.

History books tell us that he then formed a secret society of the Nine Just Men to keep science underground, after which time atomic and other weapons of mass destruction disappeared from the world stage until our Dr. Frankensteinian scientists brought the nuclear monster to life in 1945 at Trinity Site in New Mexico.

How does this relate to Atlantis? There is, among a few modern Hindu historians, speculation that the Indian thousand-city trading empire, now part of the great Rajasthan Desert in northern India, had mercantile outposts in different parts of the world. A good guess for one of them is an island in the Pacific, one thousand miles west of Chile off the coast of South America, the mysterious Easter Island. European ship captains, when they discovered the island in the 1700s, reported that many of the natives were white skinned and had brown, and yes, even red hair. And to complete the worldwide linkup, Easter Island has the same glued-together stonework, identical to walls in both Peru and Northern India. Bones from the graves of Easter Island display a DNA pattern consistent with Europoids; 60 percent Europoids, in fact.

Their written alphabet, Rongorongo, is made up of human-like stick figures, which no one has interpreted to date. However, linguists know two other locations for the stick figures: the ruins of Mohenjo Daro in Pakistan (formerly India), and similar stick-figure writings show up in early Chinese (see Jean-Michel Schwartz, *The Secrets of Easter Island*, 1979). However, present-day Chinese scholars strongly dispute this.

If the Hindus had established worldwide trading connections, did they butt heads with the Atlanteans? Perhaps the Greek philosopher Plato can tell us, for he describes a million-man Atlantean grand army that was defeated by the ancient Hellenes, ancestors of the modern Greeks. The Atlanteans were aggressively pursuing a world empire, Plato wrote, and quite likely this would have brought them into conflict with a Hindu trading empire. War! A war that the Mahabharata tells us the Hindus won, aided, of course, by their technology and their testosterone-fueled personalities.

Dramatization-speculation: The Hindu army planned to use speed and shock to defeat the Atlantean self-defense force. The planners, back in India, had psyched out their enemy and believed the Atlanteans were suckers for new Hindu tactics and secret weapons. The new weapons were the motorcycle, powered by an external combustion engine, which in centuries to come would be reinvented; and the newly invented black powder rifles. (Alexander of Macedon, while storming an Indian city, was shot in the chest by a firearm.) The inventors had developed strong, synthetic flexible tires, so the bikes could travel off the roads and hit the enemy where least expected. Surprise would throw the stolid, obedient Atlanteans into the one situation they were psychologically unprepared for: the need to improvise and fight as individuals. While they were extremely brave, they obediently fought best when fighting for the gods. The people of Atlantis believed that their rulers were, in fact, kinsmen of the gods. They became disillusioned, just as many thousands of years later the Incan army fell apart in Peru when their emperor, Atahualpa, failed to rise up as predicted on the third day after being strangled by the Spanish soldiers, thus convincing the Incan soldiers they had been abandoned by heaven. Like the excellent soldiers they were, they fought valiantly, but they had lost heart.

Speculation: On Atlantis, the bike soldiers were landed on a remote, unprotected section of the coast by the new radar-invisible IFOs. The entire advance raiding party consisted of only ten thousand men, battle-hardened volunteers, and they were prepared to take on all ten nations of Atlantis. Their objective was to seize the communication centers, kill the leaders, and black out the country by destroying the terrible firestone laser stations, which had the power to shoot down invading Hindu aircraft. Destroying the firestone lasers would clear the path for the main Hindu army to land and subdue the ten nations of Atlantis, one nation at a time. Speed and surprise. The Hindu soldiers with night goggles roared toward the capital of Atlantis, and by the time the Atlanteans had collected their wits, it was too late. They were being shot down in droves. Atlantean soldiers fought bravely with their bows and arrows, deadly sling stones, spears, and war clubs, but they were no match for black powder Indian rifles. The Indians, using plans supplied by the excellent Hindu spy service, went directly to the beehive-shaped domes housing the terrible firestone lasers and put them out of action with carefully placed gunpowder charges. Other units roared to the white marble senate building, roared up the massive marble steps, and rode into parliament, which was sitting in emergency session, trying to assemble a plan to protect the motherland now that the emperor's million-man army had been crushed by the Hellenes in the Mediterranean valley. The Hindu spies were good, the intelligence was superb, and their timing was on target. The leaders of all ten Atlantean nations were present. The invaders, according to plan, methodically gunned down the senators and kept firing until there was no more movement, except a dozen or two wounded senators flopping in their gore. Shoot to kill was the plan. A few senators hid under their benches and screamed in terror and rage. Soon it was all over. The marble senate floors were running with blood. The old Atlantis was finished.

Then the main army of India landed to secure the country. The large Atlantean army quickly melted away, retreating in panic when they learned that their godlike leaders were dead. A few units fled to the mountains and reorganized under their capable officers, but although they fought to the death, they didn't have a chance. Nothing could withstand the terrible firepower of rifles and the shock of being outmaneuvered by lightning-fast motorcycles.

The Hindu political officers selected docile Atlantean aristocrats to replace the assassinated senators, and the native bureaucrats soon had Atlantis running smoothly again. The obedient people of Atlantis soon settled in and began worshipping the Hindus as the new gods. Later, over the many thousands of years, they colonized the country to their southwest—the Americas—they built great cities in what is now Brazil, which would become ruins when tectonic plates collided, emptying the gigantic Amazonian inland freshwater sea and raising up the Andes mountain range, thus creating a barrier to the westward flowing rain clouds. It rained, seemingly forever.

The great Amazonian river system and newly created rain forest made life miserable for the survivors, and the mixture of Aryan-Atlanteans who survived moved from the jungles and up into the Andes to create the many sophisticated nations that the Incas consolidated into their empire.

Many more thousands of years later, Aryan-Atlantis once again collided with the mother civilization in India. Another high-tech world war broke out, which ended with the sinking of Atlantis and the start of the fabled Fimbul winter that lasted for several years without interruption. After the terrible winter ended, the survivors set about seeing that nuclear war would never happen again. Thus began the outlawing of technology and science. This is the background and motive for the hiding of Crespi's artifacts in the dank caves and tunnels of the Amazon.

Fact: The Incan leader Pachacuti the Fourth was told by his wife-sister that she had a dream that some fearsome men were coming. They would be riding strange beasts, have terrible thunder weapons that vomited flames, and would be covered with hair, especially on their faces. To the Incas with their smooth, hairless faces, the anticipated bearded visitors must have sounded both frightening and weird. Further, she told Pachacuti, they would be wearing shiny metal clothing that would repel Incan weapons. Then she said the gods told her that her husband must destroy all writing and obliterate their history. The troubled Incan immediately complied, which is just one reason why we don't know the true history of our world. During the civil war between Atahualpa and Huascar, both sides eagerly burned even the knotted-string Quipu records, which could have been used to retell Incan history. The enemy soldiers killed the memorizers of Quipu and burned the Quipu storehouses, so the Spanish weren't the only ones setting fire to history.

Years later, when Francisco Pizarro arrived with one hundred foot soldiers, a few dinky cannons, and only sixty or seventy horsemen, they were met by Huayna Capac, an Incan ruler who was reportedly so gentle that he could refuse nothing honorable to any woman who asked, regardless of her age or status. Knowing the prophetic dream had come true, the mild-mannered Huayna Capac lay down and died, some say of despair.

His death sparked a brutal and ferocious war of succession, in which one of his sons, the capable Atahualpa prevailed, but in so doing caused such chaos that it broke the back of the Incan empire. Pizarro was there to take advantage of the chaos and of Atahualpa's naive, arrogant curiosity, for Atahualpa, wanting to see if he could make use of the strangers, and not knowing how ferocious they were or how desperately they wanted the nation's gold, welcomed them with open arms. In one afternoon of slaughter they brutally kidnapped him, killing at least seven thousand of his unarmed followers, the cream of Incan nobility. They later offered him a choice: become a Christian or be burned at the stake. Once he was baptized, they strangled him and seized the empire.

TIME AND
THE ATOMIC LATTE

THE ANCIENT HINDUS were not so weird, really; they just experienced time differently from the way we do, from their brief *truti* of one millionth of a second to the staggering count of the *mahamanvantara* of 311.04 trillion years. And they saw it in circles. Circles were, for them, the key factor. Time circled itself, they believed, and what started at a point in space continued in a never-ending circle until it met itself where it had begun. The *rishi* (holy scholars) of ancient India invented a symbol for time—the serpent swallowing its tail. One great advantage with a circle is the lack of any final ending. With the end of the World Age prophesized by the ancient Mayans in 2012 fast approaching, we would do well to adopt the Hindu view.

While on the European-African side of the world the scholar Augustine (340–430 CE) was a powerful early church leader, Bishop of Hippo in North Africa, perhaps the most influential Christian since Paul of Tarsus, was teaching that time was a straight line with a beginning and an end. He prepared us for Charles Darwin's linear view of evolution. We crawled from the slime of chaos and have been progressing in a straight line, which, in a logical extension of this thinking, will eventually end in a big whimper when everything runs out of energy and collapses into the end of time. The Hindu circle of time is much more elegant, and there is overwhelming evidence that they had a high and powerful science—a science culminating in nuclear bombs and the means to deliver them. Rockets and flying craft are described in Hindu history books and scientific texts in such detail that they could be reconstructed today, and quite likely are.

The brilliant scholar and philosopher Sri Aurobindu Ghosh (1872–1950) wrote, "European scholarship regards human civilization as a recent progression starting yesterday with the Fiji islander, and ending today with a Rockefeller, conceiving ancient culture as necessarily half-savage. It is a superstition of modern thought that the march of knowledge has always been linear. Our vision of prehistory is terribly inadequate. We have not yet rid our minds from the hold of a one and only God or one and only book, and now a one and only science."

For instance, U.S. Col. Henry Olcott, cofounder with Helena P. Blavatsky of the Theosophical Society, wrote in 1881, "The ancient Hindus could navigate the air, and not only navigate it, but fight battles in it like so many war eagles combating for the domination of the clouds. To be so perfect in aeronautics, they must have known all the arts and science, including the strata and the currents of the atmosphere, the relative temperature, humidity, and density of the various gases."

Frederick Soddy (1877–1956) was an English scientist who worked with the famous scientist Rutherford at McGill University in Canada and was awarded a Nobel Prize in 1921 for his contributions to the knowledge of the chemistry of radioactive substances. Soddy thought highly of the ancient Hindu Mahayana and Mahabharata. In his book *The Interpretation of Radium,* published in 1909, he wrote, "I believe that there have been civilizations in the past that were familiar with atomic energy, and that by misusing it they were totally destroyed."

Even J. Robert Oppenheimer, who played a key role in developing the atom bomb, when asked if the bomb at Alamagordo was the first one to be exploded is said to have answered, "Well, yes. In modern times, of course."

The Hindu Mahabharata, thought to have been assembled well over three thousand years ago from incalculable older documents states, "A blazing shaft of light possessed of the effulgence of a smokeless fire was let off . . . The survivors lost their nails and hair and their food became unfit for eating. For several subsequent years the sun, the stars, and the sky remained shrouded with clouds and bad weather." This weapon was known as the weapon of Brahma, or the flame of Indra.

The Indian sacred books say:

Subdue the earth and all that is in it. Oh disciple, sail in oceans in steamers, fly in the air in airplanes, know God the creator through the Vedas, control thy breath through yoga, through astronomy know functions of day and night, know all the Vedas: Rig, Yajur, Sama, and Atharva. Through astronomy, geography, and geology, go thou to all the different countries of the world under the sun. Mayest thou attain through good preaching to statesmanship and artisanship, through medical science obtain knowledge of all medicinal plants, through hydrostatics learn the different uses of water, through electricity understand the working of ever lustrous lightning.

YAJUR VEDA, VERSE 6.21

O royal skilled engineer, construct sea-boats propelled on water by our experts, and airplanes, moving and flying upward, after the clouds that reside in the mid-region, that fly as the boats move on the sea, that fly high over and below the watery clouds. Be thou, thereby, prosperous in this world created by the omnipresent God.

YAJUR VEDA, VERSE 10.19

And how about this:

> The atomic energy fissions the ninety-nine elements, covering its path by the bombardment of neutrons. Desirous of stalking the head, that is, the chief part of the swift power hidden in the mass of molecular adjustments of the elements, this atomic energy approaches it in the very act of fissioning it by the above-noted bombardment.
>
> ATHARVA VEDA, VERSES 20.41

The *Rig Veda*, considered by many scholars to be the oldest surviving document in the world has this to say in verse 9.14.1: "A Jalavan is a craft built to operate in the air."

Additionally in verse 3.14.1, "Kaara operates on ground and water."

And in verse 4.36.1, "Trichakra is a craft of three stories."

MERCURY-POWERED AIRCRAFT

A *vayu* is a gas-powered aircraft. A gas-powered aircraft is mentioned in other Hindu books, such as the Sama Negara Sutradara. It goes like this:

> In a stout iron box, carefully welded, place mercury and put "the fire" under it. When the mercury gets hot it turns to gas and the *vimana* (Sanskrit for "flying craft") ascends with a terrible roar.

A bright young scientist named Henry Monteith, who worked at Sandia Laboratories in the Southwest, shared his conclusions about the Hindu mercury engine. He had given much thought to the mercury craft, and he thought it an extremely doable concept. Monteith pointed out that gasified mercury would be an extremely efficient turbine propellant. Heated mercury, which quickly gasifies from the liquid state in a "strongly welded, sealed container," would develop tremendous pressure and when jetted from the box at very high speed would exert force against the iron blades of an enclosed inner turbine, causing it to spin a shaft. The mercury vapor, when exhausted from the closed system turbine, would be cooled through a cold water condenser and immediately condense back into its original liquid form and recycle without loss of the propellant mercury. The smaller, mercury-propelled turbine blades, turning a shaft attached to a larger turbine on the other end of the shaft, would then spin the blades, which would, somewhat like our modern turbo fans, develop powerful thrust. Henry Monteith was convinced that the Indian engineers had actually built a vimana from the design description he read. The mercury motor had another advantage; the mercuric gas wouldn't touch the iron turbine blades it pushed against because of the repellant electrostatic charge. Only electrons would impinge on the blades, friction free, making the motor very efficient, and as the writers described it, the outer, larger turbine, pumping air, would cause the craft to ascend with a great roar. I asked Henry Monteith if he thought we were making such craft today somewhere on earth. He didn't answer.

There are plenty of other descriptions of Hindu technology. For instance the Kathasaritsagara text mentions two skilled engineers and woodworkers named Rajyadhara and Pranadhara, who built an ocean-crossing ship. The two men also manufactured an aircraft that could carry a thousand passengers. Obviously the men were engineers as well as skilled woodworkers, and perhaps even prosperous factory owners. Science fiction? I doubt it. Especially when you consider the matter-of-fact way these inventions are described and the great wealth of details supplied, and the opinions of quite a few modern scientists.

The rocket-delivered atomic weapons described in the Mahabharata reduced to ashes the entire race of the Vrishnis and the Andhakas. The corpses were so burned as to be unrecognizable. Hair and nails fell out. Pottery broke without apparent cause, and the birds turned white. After a few hours foodstuffs were infected. To escape from this fire the soldiers threw themselves in rivers to wash themselves and their equipment.

There is mention also that the Hindu flying ships circled the globe and had regular land stops at such places as Easter Island, which is a thousand miles from the west coast of South America, home of the giant Moa-Moa statues. But there is someone living on Easter Island who can fill in a big gap in our story. He is Pakarati the sculptor, who was interviewed by Thor Heyerdal. Pakarati carved strange Kava statues, which Heyerdal photographed for his book, *Kon-Tiki.* Pakarati told Heyerdal that he carved these statues exactly as his father had taught him, and Pakarati's father had made him swear an oath not to change any details because it was very important, but he didn't know why. The wooden Kava statues display thick goitered necks, swollen stomachs, emaciated ribs, and the signs of radiation sickness. The Kava statues tie into the Mahabharata epic of India, which describes, rather accurately, the gruesome symptoms of radiation poisoning.

There is another connection to a worldwide Aryan empire, the Rongorongo boards with their carvings of stick figures that are mirror images to the very ancient Rongorongo writing found at the destroyed city of Mohenjo Daro in Pakistan. This was an amazingly well-planned city with a sophisticated sewage system, better than most sewage disposal in a large part of India and Pakistan today, and it is now one of the more dangerously radioactive sites in the world.

Archaeologists found round blobs of blackened glass in the ruins, and the bones of skeletons among the ruins were exceptionally radioactive. The blobs of glass were a puzzle, however, until one scientist discovered it was pottery that had been vitrified by an exceptionally high heat.

But there is another puzzle here: There were very few skeletons. The city was almost empty. Had the enemy, with a chivalry we have forgotten, warned the city that an iron thunderbolt was on its way, allowing them time to escape? Did the Mohenjo Daro intelligence service warn of the impending attack? There was just one group of twenty-seven people at the end of one street, and a few scattered about the rest of the city. Were they looters or just stubborn?

Now back to Father Crespi. The bronze plaque he was so fond of shows artistic sophistication and features Aryan Caucasian faces. That, plus the examples of science and technology, aluminum wall coverings, extremely hard copper that corrodes into a black patina, and the tenacious metallic glue all strengthen the idea of white people, Aryan Hindus, bringing technology to South America.

THE
DOOMSDAY DEVICE

FROM AN ANCIENT ARYAN-HINDU document comes one brief episode in the war for world domination.

It was like a scene from the classic movie *Dr. Strangelove*. A nasty man named Asvattha-varm fled the battlefield of Kurukshetra in India after his troops were destroyed by the hero Arjuna's army, which was aided by the supernatural guidance of Krishna, Arjuna's friend and chariot driver. The Mahabharata, which is many times longer than the *Iliad* and the *Odyssey* combined, tells of an exciting, terrifying, wild, and earth-straddling global war; a war, fortunately for us, which the good guys won. It tells of the battle between the IFOs of the evil Asvins (Atlantis) and the vimanas (aircraft) of the Hindus, including a battle between them on the moon.

Let's get back to Mr. Nasty, Asvattha-varm. He and two of his buddies fled the battlefield where millions had been slaughtered on both sides, and Asvattha-varm vowed to punish the victorious Arjuna and his army. He would sneak up on them in the middle of the night, catch them sleeping, and destroy them with his special "magic" weap-

110

ons. This was particularly bad because the strict Hindu military code forbade a warrior from taking advantage of a sleeping enemy. However, Krishna had predicted that both armies would be destroyed. This civil war, the Mahabharata tells us, was fought for the possession of Earth, but it offers a confusing description of the weapons used. The writer confusedly jumbles together swordplay and nuclear rockets. It tells of Mr. Nasty killing the sleeping enemy one at a time with a sword, and then again it hints that he destroyed many hundreds of thousands of victorious soldiers with some sort of "magical" weapon. Then, it says, he launched the much-feared Brahma-siras missile, the Doomsday Machine, at Arjuna. But there was one little problem for Arjuna and Krishna: Asvattha-varm knew how to launch it but didn't know how to recall it. The text mentions that he recited a "launch" mantra. Hindu holy men and women claim that a mantra is a precisely crafted set of commands or mathematical formulas that allow the adept to control the very gods, angels, and archangels who animate all natural force with their will and thought power.

Krishna and Arjuna became aware of the Brama-sira-astra launching and reversed the mantric launch code, shutting it down just barely in time. It was said that this weapon was nearly impossible to recall and was capable of setting off an atomic chain reaction and incinerating all life. Further evidence of a *Star Wars* scenario is the admonition that this weapon must never be used on humans, for even if it were blocked by a defensive missile, another Brama-sira rocket, it would dry up the rains, interfere with the hydrologic cycle, and produce great drought for twelve years in the entire kingdom; that is, instant global warming. Since the books hint that the kingdom was worldwide, a long-lasting drought would kill most of the people on Earth. It sounds a little crazy, but traces of that science can be discovered in India and in Latin America.

Start with the Mahabharata and Mahayana story. Then go to Mohenjo Daro near the city of Sindh, Pakistan. Long ago, Mohenjo Daro was a key world-trading center, yet United Nations and Pakistani archaeologists aren't allowed to dig there today, ostensibly because the site is contaminated with radiation. The frustrated scientists have been blocked by the military. Why? Any evidence of nuclear war in the past might be a strong influence on the politics of Pakistan, and might affect Islamic perceptions of the holy Qu'ran, which doesn't mention nuclear war.

And what of the fundamentalist mind-set of the imams, some of whom are actively trying to subvert Pakistan's government while just itching to get their hands on Pakistan's nuclear weapons for their very dangerous agenda? It is said that there are a thousand abandoned cities in the deserts of northern India, Pakistan, and surrounding countries, waiting for the archaeological spade. These ancient cities, which once belonged to the ancient trading empire of India, include Harappa, Mohenjo Daro's sister city, which also show evidence of having been nuked. There is also a quarter-mile wide, vitrified crater in the center of Harappa, which is highly radioactive and mysteriously similar to the craters at both Mohenjo Daro and Trinity Site in New Mexico. Balls of black melted pottery have also been found in the ruins. And, sadly, highly radioactive skeletons have been found. A few Indian scholars think that ancient India was the most heavily populated portion of the world in those days. Artfully engineered streets laid out in grids, indoor toilets with comfortable wooden seats, and well-designed underground sewage systems that date back to at least 3500 BCE reveal the engineering talents of these ancient people. And although it's disputed by the Chinese, their sophisticated Rongorongo writing, made up of human "stick" figures, may have been the precursor of the earliest Chinese language.

15

ROCKET ATTACK

THUNDER AND LIGHTNING rumbled and flashed in the early morning of July 16, 1945, when the final test was to be made. The bomb was carefully mounted on a steel tower. More than five miles away, scientists lay flat listening breathlessly to the time signals being announced over the radio: Minus fifteen minutes . . . minus fourteen minutes . . . minus thirteen minutes . . ." At "minus forty-five seconds" a robot mechanism took over the controls. Suddenly a giant ball of fire rose as though from the bowels of the earth, then a pillar of purple fire ten-thousand-feet high shooting skyward. The flash lit up every crevasse and ridge of the San Andres Mountains. Then it shot higher to forty thousand feet, a huge rainbow-colored ball transforming swiftly to mushroom shape. It was lit from within by lightning-like flashes and accompanied by a tremendous sustained roar. In Albuquerque, one hundred and twenty miles away, the sky blazed noonday-bright. When it was done, the tower had completely vaporized. There was only a crater a quarter-mile wide lined with melted rock and sand.

That is an eyewitness version of the first modern atomic explosion, described by James A. Crutchfield in *It Happened in New Mexico*. But there is solid evidence that it was not the first time that humans used nuclear weapons on one another.

The ancient quarter-of-a-mile crater in Mohenjo Daro, Pakistan, eerily matches the Trinity, New Mexico, bombsite and it is, more or less, the same size, with a sea of melted glass and rock covering the craters of both. There is no doubt that Mohenjo Daro was nuked.

FICTION

The following is a fictional scenario based on conjectures and suppositions, any or all of which may be accurate.

The enemy's iron thunderbolts, nuclear-tipped rockets, easily slipped through the defenses of Atlantis, almost as if the defensive, radar-operated laser cannon beams were soft butter. "What is happening?" thought Djxiactun Gupta, six foot six, heavily muscled, and a chocolate addict. (He drank three dozen cups of the perfumed, bitter, theobromine-laced drink daily.) He was military self-defense commander of the western defense zone, which extended for one thousand miles in a great sheathed ring of protection. The great Bimini self-defense circle covered the most important part of Atlantis, and it wasn't designed to fail. "By Poseidon, we are going to get hit."

Meanwhile, the Hindu rockets edged frighteningly closer. Gupta's light green fluorescent display screen showed the blips getting larger, and his computer told him they were going to hit target within ten minutes. The display told him that Bimini, the administrative, financial, and religious center of the new Aryan Atlantis, was the target, and he was on Bimini. He ordered his assistant to begin high-tuning the great sun-pumped laser cannons. He knew the designers never intended to release their full power as he was now preparing to do. But the beams of concentrated light were bouncing off the rockets and the rockets kept coming. The power of these cannons could split the earth right down the middle and release, well, who knows what forces? Scientist-military commander Gupta had never believed, not really believed, his university teachers that the earth could be destroyed completely by high-tuning the laser weapons. As he had said to himself many times in the past, "Maybe a volcano or two would go off, perhaps a major earthquake; a small price to pay for saving the most precious civilization on earth." The tuning needle was pointing into the bright crimson-red range when the warning klaxon honked out its terrible cry, "Aaarruuggghhhaa, aaarruugghhhaa." The technicians looked at one another with fear. One technician named Xibalba, with bright red hair, a fiery temper, and an independent attitude, believed his teachers and pleaded, "Sir, shut it down. Shut it down." The scientist ignored him. Xibalba pushed the scientist out of the way and seized the tuning handle, but when Gupta's powerful fist crashed into the base of his skull, he fell, heavy as a lump of lead, to the floor. The scientist screamed at the other technicians, "Better risk destruction than positively get wiped out by atomic rockets. Get back to your posts. Arm the lasers. Prepare to fire."

Meanwhile the tuning mechanism began to shake ominously and give off an overheated glow. The circle of vibrations went out in a deadly sphere high above them and deep down into the never-before-seen mantle of the earth where it touched with its powerful fingers a gigantic pocket of methane gas. The gas exploded, taking the way of least pressure, upward—exiting into Bimini. The explosion tore its way past the earth's crust carrying millions of tons of white-hot magma, which totally destroyed the self-defense complex and vomited lava in a deadly circle as far away as the great forests of Sweden and Finland, leaving a gaping, seething hollow. The nuclear rockets were disintegrated. There was a brief pause, and then the surrounding ocean water crashed into the hollow and hit the magma with all its fury. Many miles of ocean water poured into the hole where it contacted fresh magma, and when the weight of the seawater reached critical mass it exploded again, relentlessly following the coast of the Atlantic island with explosion after explosion. This took a complete day, twenty-four hours, and it blew out from under the giant island thousands of square miles of the very underpinnings of Atlantis. The explosions shook the entire world and were felt as far away as Asia. And the island settled slowly into the hollow space, and the oceans waters rolled relentlessly over Atlantis. Dead were more than a hundred million people. From the "isles of the blessed" it became the "isles of the dead."

The preceding is pure science fiction but it is based in a few scattered facts, racial memories, folk tales, the readings of Edgar Cayce and Annie Besant, Plato, and the *Oera Linda Boek.*

How did our ancestors survive the terrible Ice Age caused by the sinking of Atlantis? Have you tried frozen wooly mammoth? Wooly mammoths have been unearthed in Siberia and eaten. One scientist said it tasted like good aged beef, and slaves mining gold at the brutal Soviet mines of Siberia also dug up and ate similar mammoths.

World legends tell that after some great catastrophe people turned to cannibalism. The Mahabharata tells of ancient Hindu atomic weapons and flying craft. European literature tells of Atland, a sunken continent peopled with great magicians (read scientists). Solon, the great lawgiver of Athens, visited the Egyptians and brought back the story of Atlantis disappearing in "a single day and a single night, it disappeared beneath the waves."

And of course the bronze plaques from Crespi's treasure show us what Atlantean colonists look like. They had Caucasian features. There is one plaque showing a button-nosed man who would be quite at home in Ireland.

The technology, the glue, the aluminum wall covering, and all the rest tells us it came from a scientific empire—Hindu Atlantis.

The preceding events neatly stitch some of the facts together to make a coherent and believable mosaic. It could have happened that way. And if it did, why don't we know about these earth-shaking events?

Suppose the few survivors—starving, grief-stricken, numb with cold, living in constant terror of marauding cannibals—made a decision to never, never go back to world-destroying weapons. Never. And suppose when the sun finally began to shine, the ecologists and greens gained power in the newly formed councils. Outlaw technology and outlaw science. Create a Stone Age. The survivors would listen with grim attention and, essential to the plan, wipe out our history and begin again. From the caves of refuge they emerged as cave men and women. Not the cartoon brutes dragging their women by the hair, but thoroughly civilized humans, ready to begin again.

16

THE FIMBUL WINTER

FACT: A SUDDEN ICE AGE descended on the world. Geologists make an educated guess as to the dates. There were other ice ages, with ten-thousand-year warming periods between, but the one that concerns us here coincided, more or less, with the guessed sinking of Atlantis about 11,000 years ago, and the geologically recorded ocean level rise.

The Dutch *Oera Linda Boek* reveals:

We baked our bread with the sun and the weather was beautiful, there was much singing and we were living quite happy. Then the climate changed abruptly. It got cold, very, very cold, and quickly. The thing that frightened people was the suddenness of the horrible, icy onslaught. One day it was sunny and warm, and the very next day, relentless snow; thousands of cubic miles of ocean water turned into live steam, and the water vapor turned to snow as a hole was blasted in our protective atmosphere, and the cold of space rushed in. Instant winter, called, in Scandinavia, the terrible Fimbulvetr, the Fimbul winter.

Perhaps the following will resonate with you.

DRAMATIZATION-SPECULATION

First came the quick, icy blasts of wind and then snow, never-ending snow. Most of our people froze to death or were killed by cannibal foreigners; and our animals, cattle, sheep, and goats died, for there was no pasture. There were no log homes to protect us, just flimsy ones built for warm, sunny weather. It was not nice. The few of us who lived near caves fled to them only to find them occupied by animals. This was good fortune for us, though a few of us died fighting them; we ate their meat and lived. And later on we learned to use their hides for clothing. We managed to get a fire going, and we survived. The freeze came so quickly that large herds of mammoth and bison and other animals simply disappeared under the snow. Later we trained our dogs to find the frozen graveyards. The animals froze so quickly that their meat was good to eat, no matter how many years had passed, and we survived. We learned that we must be vigilant, for bands of cannibal-foreigners were on the prowl. They were starving, and they looked on us as dinner. We had to remain alert and keep our spears and bows by our side. This was the Fimbul winter, and we wondered if the world would ever get warm again; if we would ever again smell a flower or bite into a fresh, delicious apple. Oh, how we longed for fresh food.

For years and years we sat around the campfire and tried to understand what had happened to the world. Endless debate. We suspected that atomic weapons were the cause. The two world-controlling nations, Bahrata in northern India and Asvin in the Atlantic Ocean, had hundreds of nuclear weapons, and we knew they had used them. These weapons might have been the cause of this terrible Fimbul winter. We vowed that if the winter ended, some day we would find out what had happened and put a stop to this madness. We must unite the world, outlaw science and technology, and see that this never occurs again. We must start again at the Stone Age level. Retain our mathematics and healing arts, retain our language and poetry, and above all retain our belief in the Divine Father-Mother and her children, our parents, the gods.

After many, many years it gradually warmed, and eventually people emerged from their caves. The cities of northern India were still radioactive and became places of taboo. The entire structure of civilization had collapsed, and the survivors began slowly and painfully communicating again. We remembered enough technology to build huge, crude gasbag airships; we flew the world, locating other survivors. We organized under the banner "Never again." Find the books; burn, hide, or bury the technology. Form vigorous secret, armed political action groups to prevent people from developing science and to outlaw technology. Some of us thought that persuasion was the way to deal with scientists; others, more practical, simply killed them.

FACT

The Indian king who launched the iron thunderbolt and destroyed two separate societies of people many thousands of years after the Fimbul winter ended selected nine men, each of whom had a scientific specialty. Each collected all the information on his area of expertise and quite likely destroyed all copies of documents except his encyclopedias, which he hid from the public.

A perfect example of this is "Bishop Freddie," an authentic ordained bishop who studied magic. I invited him to visit me in Miami, to test his theories. He brought a small bag of herbs to make a "black wand," a wand made of plants and herbs carefully wrapped in tar tape, and told me that it was used to locate north. Freddie explained that the old book he'd studied said the wand should be coated with tar, but he found that black tar tape did just as well. We put it in a tub of water and it pointed north. I told Freddie he had to teach me how to do that. "Oh, no way, Rich," he answered. "I took a solemn oath to teach only one other person, and that person had to be my pupil and swear to maintain the line of secrecy. You could never be my pupil, and you love to share stories, so no."

This was my first hint that there is a secret substratum of knowledge from antiquity, carefully protected by an unbroken line of initiation. Bishop Freddie and the previously mentioned Nine Just Men from India suggest there are secret repositories of underground science assembled after the Fimbul winter.

In Blavatsky's *Secret Doctrine* she tells of a brotherhood and sisterhood of adepts who have access to this confidential information. One example is Brother Koot Hoomi of Kashmir, northern India. In one of his *Letters of the Masters of the Wisdom* to A. P. Sinnett, Koot Hoomi revealed some of the hidden knowledge. Sinnett was the influential publisher of the English-Indian newspaper *Pioneer,* who in 1882 wanted to recruit for the long-term goal of freeing India.

And of course India, inspired by Gandhi, freed itself peacefully in 1949.

Koot Hoomi told of Indian secret science, and explained way back in 1880 that rain could be induced chemically, that the planets give off more heat than they can possibly receive from the sun, and that, "You will hear the sounds from the distant stars before you see them. This is a prediction." That prediction was validated in the next century with the radio telescope, and in the 1950s, Jupiter was discovered to be, indeed, emitting more heat than it could get from the sun.

The letters of Koot Hoomi can be read today, and they are carefully preserved on microfilm by the British Museum. Koot Hoomi, by the way, is the teacher who taught Annie Besant and her friend, Bishop Charles Webster Leadbeater, the art of interdimensional seeing.

CONCLUSION

THE PRESENCE OF THE Crespi artifacts—steel-hard copper wheels that won't distort under high speed; metallurgically pure aluminum "wallpaper;" the multicontinental metallic glue holding buildings together in what was once northern India, Latin America, and Easter Island; the El Panecillo laser building; the nuclear-damaged sites of Mohenjo Daro and Harrapa in Pakistan; Pakarati's Easter Island wood carvings showing radiation victims; and the marble temple ruins in the Bahamas all tell us of ancient civilizations ruined by cataclysm and the human hand.

The gold wall decoration depicting sad, obviously genetic malengineered half-humans morosely staring at us are terrible reminders that the murderously competitive games we allow the super-rich and powerful to play usually have painful and tragic consequences. All the while they dangle shiny, sugarcoated, dangerous, frightfully expensive and ugly schemes before us. And all the while we continue to grab at the bait.

As Herman Melville said in "Bartleby the Scrivener," "Ah, humanity!"

CRITIAS

CRITIAS IS ONE OF THE dialogs written by Plato around 360 BCE. It is important because it is one of the earliest references to Atlantis in world literature.

In *Critias,* Plato's great-grandfather describes to Socrates the ancient knowledge of the origin, physical description, government, and decline of Atlantis. The translation that appears below is from *Atlantis: The Antediluvian World* by Ignatius Donnelly (New York: Harper & Brothers, 1882).

But in addition to the gods you have mentioned, I would specially invoke Mnemosyne (Memory), for all the important part of what I have to tell is dependent on her favor, and if I can recollect and recite enough of what was said by the priests and brought hither by Solon, I doubt not that I shall satisfy the requirements of this theatre. To that task, then, I will address myself.

Let me begin by observing, first of all, that nine thousand was the sum of years that had elapsed since the war, which was said to have taken place between those who dwelt outside the Pillars of Hercules and those who dwelt within them: this war I am now to describe. Of the combatants, on the one side the city of Athens was reported to have been the ruler and to have directed the contest; the combatants on the other side were led by the kings of the islands of Atlantis, which, as I was saying, once had an extent greater than that of Libya and Asia; and when afterward sunk by an earthquake, became an impassable barrier of mud to voyagers sailing from hence to the ocean. The progress of the history will unfold the various tribes of barbarians and Greeks that then existed, as they successively appear on the scene. But I must begin by describing, first of all, the Athenians as they were in that day, and their enemies who fought with them; and I shall have to tell of the power and form of government of both of them. Let us give the precedence to Athens . . .

Many great deluges have taken place during the nine thousand years, for that is the number of years that have elapsed since the time of which I am speaking. And in all the ages and changes of things there has never been any settlement of the earth flowing down from the mountains, as in other places, which is worth speaking of; it has always been carried around in a circle and disappeared in the depths below. The consequence is that in comparison to what then was, there are remaining in small islets only the bones of the wasted body, as they may be called, all the richer and softer parts of the soil having fallen away, and the mere skeleton of the country being left . . .

And next, if I have not forgotten what I heard when I was a child, I will impart to you the character and origin of their adversaries; for friends should not keep their stories to themselves, but have them in common. Yet, before proceeding farther in the narrative, I ought to warn you that you must not be surprised should you hear Greek names given to foreigners. I will tell the reason of this: Solon, who was intending to use the tale for his poem, made an investigation into the meaning of the names and found that the early Egyptians, in writing them down, had translated into their own language, and he recovered the meaning of the several names and retranslated them, and copied them out again in our language. My grandfather Dropidas had the original writing, which is still in my possession and was carefully studied by me when I was a child. Therefore, if you hear names such as are used in this country, you must not be surprised, for I have told you the reason of them.

The tale, which was of great length, began as follows: I have before remarked in speaking to the gods that they divided the whole earth amongst themselves in portions differing in extent, and made for themselves temples and sacrifices. And Poseidon, receiving for his lot the island of Atlantis, begat children by a mortal woman and settled in part of the island, which I will proceed to describe. On the side toward the sea, and in the center of the whole island, there was a plain, which is said to have been the fairest of all plains, and very fertile. Near the plain again, and also in the center of the island at a distance of about fifty stadia, there was a mountain, not very high on any side. In this mountain there dwelt one of the earth-born primeval men of that country, whose name was Euenor, and he had a wife named Leukippe, and they had an only daughter, who was named Cleito. The maiden was growing up to womanhood when her father and mother died. Poseidon fell in love with her and had intercourse with her; and breaking the ground, enclosed the hill in which she dwelt all round, making alternate zones of sea and land, larger and smaller, encircling one with a lathe out of the center of the island, equidistant every way, so that no man could get to the island, for ships and voyages were not heard of. He himself, as he was a god, found no difficulty in making special arrangements nor the center island, bringing two streams of water under the earth, which he caused to ascend as springs, one of warm water and the other of cold, and making every variety of food to spring up abundantly in the earth. He also begat and brought up five pairs of male children, dividing the pair between his mother's dwelling and surrounding allotment, which was the largest and best, and made him king over the rest; the others he made princes and gave them rule over many men and a large territory. And he named them all. The eldest, who was king, he named Atlas, and from him the whole island and the ocean received the name Atlantic. To his twin brother, who was born after him and obtained as his lot the extremity of the island toward the Pillars of Hercules, as far as the country that is still called the region of Gades in that part of the world, he gave a name that in the Hellenic language is Eumelus; in the language of the country that is named after him, Gadeirus. Of the second part of twins he called one Ampheres and the other Euaemon. To the third part of twins he gave the name Mneseus to the older and Autocthon to the one who followed him. Of the fourth part of twins he called the elder Elasippus and the younger, Mestor. And of the fifth pair he gave to the elder the name of Azaes, and to the younger, Diaprepes. All these and their descendants were the inhabitants and rulers of divers islands in the open sea, and also, as has been already said, they held sway in the other direction over the country within the Pillars as far as Egypt and Tyrrhenia.

Now Atlas had a numerous and honorable family, and his eldest branch always retained the kingdom, which the eldest son handed on to this eldest for many generations, and they had such an amount of wealth as was never before possessed by kings and potentate, and is not likely ever to be again; and they were furnished with everything that they could have, both in city and country. For because of the greatness of their empire, many things were brought to them from foreign countries, and the island itself provided much of what was required by them for the uses of life. In the first place, they dug out of the earth whatever was to be found there, mineral as well as metal, and that which is now only a name—*aurichalcum*—was dug out of the earth in many parts of the island, and with the exception of gold, was esteemed the most precious metal among the men of those days. There was an abundance of wood for carpenters work, and sufficient maintenance for tame and wild animals. Moreover, there were a great number of elephants in the island, and there was provision for animals of every kind, both for those that live in lakes and marshes and rivers, and also for those that live in mountains and on plains, and therefore for the animal that is the largest and most voracious of them all. And also, whatever fragrant things there are in the earth, whether roots, or herbage, or woods, or distilling drops of flowers or fruits, grew and thrived in that land; and again, the cultivated fruit of the earth, both the dry edible fruit and other species of food, which we call by the general name of legumes; and the fruits having a hard rind, affording drinks and meats and ointments and good store of chestnuts and the like, which may be used to play with and are fruits that spoil with keeping; and the pleasant kinds of dessert, which console us after dinner when we are full and tired of eating—all these that sacred island lying beneath the sun brought forth from the earth, and they employed themselves in constructing their temples, palaces, harbors, and docks; and they arranged the whole country in the following manner. First of all they bridged over the zones of the sea that surrounds the ancient metropolis, and made a passage into and out of the royal palace, and then they began to build the palace in the habitation of the god and of their ancestors. This they continued to ornament in successive generations, every king surpassing the one who came before him to the utmost of his power, until they made the building a marvel to behold for size and for beauty. And beginning from the sea, they dug a canal 350 feet in width and 100 feet in depth, and fifty stadia in length, which they carried through to the outermost zone, making a passage from the sea up to this, which became a harbor, and leaving an opening sufficient to enable the largest vessels to find ingress. Moreover, they divided the zones of land, which parted the zones of sea, constructing bridges of such a width as would leave a passage for a single trireme to pass out of one into another, and roofed them over; and there was a way underneath for the ships, for banks of the zones were raised considerably above the water. Now the largest of the zones into which a passage was cut from the sea was three stadia in breadth, and the zone of land, which came next, of equal breadth; but the next two, as well the zone of water as of land, were two stadia, and the one that surrounded the central island was a stadium only in width. This island in which the palace was situated had a diameter of five stadia. This and the zones and the bridge, which was the sixth part of a stadium in width, they surrounded by a stone wall, on either side placing towers; and gates on the bridges where the sea passed in the stone, which was used in the work they quarried from underneath the center island and from underneath the zones on the outer as the inner side. One kind of stone was white, another black, and a third red; and as they quarried, they at the same time hollowed out docks double within, having roofs formed out of the native rock. Some of their buildings were simple, but in others they put together different stones, which they intermingled for the sake of ornament, to be a natural source of delight. The entire circuit of the wall, which went round the outermost one, they covered with a coating of brass; and the circuit of the next wall they coated with tin; and the third, which encompassed the citadel, flashed with the red light of aurichalcum. The palaces in the interior of the citadel were constructed in this wise: In the center was a holy temple dedicated to Cleito and Poseidon, which remained inaccessible and was surrounded by an enclosure of gold. This was the spot in which they originally begat the race of the ten princes, and thither they annually brought the fruits of the earth in their seasons from all the ten portions, and performed sacrifices to each of them. Here, too, was Poseidon's own temple, of a stadium in length and half a stadium in width, and of a proportionate height, having a sort of barbaric splendor. All the outside of the temple, with the exception of the pinnacles, they covered with silver, and the pinnacles with gold. In the interior of the temple the roof was of ivory, adorned everywhere with gold and silver and aurichalcum; all the other parts of the walls and pillars and floor they lined with aurichalcum. In the temple they placed statues of gold. There was the god himself standing in a chariot—charioteer of six winged horses—and of such a size that he touched the roof of the building with his head. Around him there were a hundred nereids (nymphs) riding on a dolphin, for such was thought to be the number of them in that day. There were also in the interior of the temple other images, which had been dedicated by private individuals. And around the temple on the outside were placed statues of gold of all the ten kings and of their wives, and there were many other great offerings, both of kings and of private individuals, coming both from the city itself and the foreign cities over which they held sway. There was an altar, too, which in size and workmanship corresponded to the rest of the work, and there were palaces in like manner, which answered to the greatness of the kingdom and the glory of the temple.

In the next place, they used fountains both of cold and hot springs; these were very abundant, and both kinds wonderfully adapted to use by reason of the sweetness and excellence of their waters. They constructed buildings about them and planted suitable trees; also cisterns, some open to the heaven, others, which they roofed over, to be used in winter as warm baths. There were the king's baths, and the baths of private persons, which were kept apart; also separate baths for women, and others again for horses and cattle, and to them they gave as much adornment as was suitable for them. From the water that ran off they carried some to the grove of Poseidon, where there were growing all manner of trees of wonderful height and beauty, owing to the excellence of the soil; the remainder was conveyed by aqueducts, which passed over the bridges to the outer circle. And there were many temples built and dedicated to many gods; also gardens and places of exercise, some for men and some set apart for horses, in both the two islands formed by the zones, and in the center of the larger of the two there was a racecourse of a stadium in width, and in length allowed to extend all round the island for horses to race in. Also there were guardhouses at intervals for the bodyguard, the more trusted of whom had their duties appointed to them in the lesser zone, which was nearer the Acropolis; while the most trusted of all had houses given them within the citadel, and about the persons of the kings. The docks were full of triremes and naval stores, and all things were quite ready for use. Enough of the plan of the royal palace.

Crossing the outer harbors, which were three in number, you would come to a wall, which began at the sea and went all round. This was everywhere fifty stadia distance from the largest zone and harbor and enclosed the whole, meeting at the mouth of the channel toward the sea. The entire area was densely crowded with habitations; and the canal and the largest of the harbors were full of vessels and merchants coming from all parts, who from their numbers, kept up a multitudinous sound of human voices and din of all sorts night and day. I have repeated his descriptions of the city and the parts about the ancient palace nearly as he gave them, and now I must endeavor to describe the nature and arrangements of the rest of the country. The whole country was described as being very lofty and precipitous on the side of the sea, but the country immediately about the surrounding city was a level plain, itself surrounded by mountains that descended toward the sea; it was smooth and even, but of an oblong shape, extending in one direction three thousand stadia, and going up the country from the sea through the center of the island two thousand stadia. The whole region of the island lies toward the south and is sheltered from the north. The surrounding mountains were celebrated for their number and size and beauty, which they exceeded all that are now to be seen anywhere; having in them also many wealthy inhabited villages, rivers, lakes, and meadows supplying food enough for every animal—wild or tame—and wood of various sorts, abundant for every kind of work.

I will describe the plain, which had been cultivated during many ages by many generations of kings. It was rectangular and for the most part straight and oblong; and what it wanted of the straight line followed the line of the circular ditch. The depth and width and length of this ditch were incredible, and gave the impression that such a work, in addition to so many other works, could hardly have been wrought by the hand of man. But I must say what I have heard. It was excavated to the depth of a hundred feet, and its breadth was a stadium everywhere; it was carried round the whole of the plain, and was ten thousand stadia in length. It received the streams that came down from the mountains, and winding round the plain, and touching the city at various points, and there let off into the sea. From above, likewise, straight canals of a hundred feet in width were cut in the plain and again let off into the ditch, toward the sea; these canals were at intervals of a hundred stadia, and by them they brought down the wood from the mountains to the city, and conveyed the fruits of the earth in ships, cutting transverse passages from one canal into another, and to the city. Twice in the year they gathered the fruits of the earth—in winter, having the benefit of the rains; and in summer, introducing the water of the canals. As to the population, each of the lots in the plain had an appointed chief of men who were fit for military service, and the size of the lot was to be a square of ten stadia each way; the total number of all the lots was sixty thousand.

And of the inhabitants of the mountains and of the rest of the country there was also a vast multitude having leaders, to whom they were assigned according to their dwellings and villages. The leader was required to furnish for war the sixth portion of a war chariot, so as to make up a total of ten thousand chariots; also two horses and riders upon them, and a light chariot without a seat accompanied by a fighting man on foot carrying a small shield, and having a chari-oteer mounted guide the horses; also, he was bound to furnish two heavy armed men, two archers, two slingers, three stone-shooters, and three javelin men, who were skirmishers, and four sailors to make up a complement of twelve hundred ships. Such was the order of war in the royal city; that of the other nine governments was different in each of them, and would be wearisome to narrate. As to offices and honors, the following was the arrangement from the first: each of the ten kings, in his own division and in his own city, had absolute control of the citizens, and in many cases of the laws, punishing and slaying whomsoever he would.

Now the relations of their governments to one another were regulated by the injunctions of Poseidon as the law had handed them down. These were inscribed by the first men on a column of aurichalcum, which was situated in the middle of the island at the temple of Poseidon, whither the people were gathered together every fifth and sixth years alternatively, this giving equal honor to the odd and to the even number. And when they were gathered together they consulted about public affairs and inquired if any one had transgressed in anything, and passed judgment on them accordingly; and before they passed judgment, they gave their pledges to one another in this wise: There were bulls who had the range of the temple of Poseidon, and the ten who were left alone in the temple, after they had offered prayers to the gods that they might take the sacrifices that were acceptable to them, hunted the bulls without weapons, but with staves and nooses; and the bull they caught they led up to the column. The victim was then struck on the head by them, and slain over the sacred inscription Now on the column; besides the law, there was inscribed an oath invoking mighty curses on the disobedient. When, therefore, after offering sacrifice according to their customs they had burnt the limbs of the bull, they mingled a cup and cast in a clot of blood for each of them. The rest of the victim they took to the fire, after having made a purification of the column all round. Then they drew from the cup in golden vessels and according to the laws on the column, and would punish any one who had previously transgressed, and that for the future they would not, if they could help, transgress any of the inscriptions and would not command or obey any ruler who commanded them to act otherwise than according to the laws of their father Poseidon. This was the prayer that each of them offered up for himself and for his family, at the same time drinking and dedicating the vessel in the temple of the god. And after spending some necessary time at supper, when darkness came on, the fire about the sacrifice was cool; all of them put on most beautiful azure robes, and sitting on the ground at night near the embers of the sacrifices on which they had sworn, and extinguishing all the fire about the temple, they received and gave judgment, if any of [these were] an accusation to bring against any one; and when they had given judgment, at daybreak they wrote down their sentences on a golden tablet and deposited them as memorials with their robes. There were many special laws, which the several kings had inscribed about the temples, but the most important was the following: that they were not to take up arms against one another and they were all to come to the rescue if any one in any city attempted to overthrow the royal house. Like their ancestors, they were to deliberate in common about war and other matters, giving supremacy to the family of Atlas; and the king was not to have the power of life and death over any of his kinsmen, unless he had the assent of the majority of the ten kings.

Such is the vast power that the god settled in the lost island of Atlantis; and this he afterward directed against our land on the following pretext, as traditions tell. For many generations, as long as the divine nature lasted in them, they were obedient to the laws and well affectioned toward the gods, who were their kinsman; for they possessed true and in every way great spirits practicing gentleness and wisdom in the various changes of life, and in their intercourse with one another. They despised everything but virtue, not caring for their present state of life and thinking lightly on the possession of gold and other property, which seemed only a burden to them; neither were they intoxicated by luxury; nor did wealth deprive them of their self control; but they were sober and saw clearly that all these goods are increased by virtuous friendship with one another and that by excessive zeal for them, and honor of them, the good of them is lost, and friendship perishes with them.

By such reflections and by the continuance in them of a divine nature, all that we have described waxed and increased in them; but when this divine portion began to fade away in them and became diluted too often, and with too much of the mortal admixture, the human nature got the upper hand; then they, being unable to bear their fortune, became unseemly, and to him who had an eye to see, they began to appear base and had lost the fairest of the precious gifts; but to those who had no eye to see true happiness, they still appeared glorious and blessed at the very time when they were filled with unrighteous avarice and power. Zeus, the god of gods, who rules with law and is able to see into such things, perceiving that an honorable race was in a most wretched state and wanting to inflect punishment on them, that they might be chastened and improved, collected all the gods into his most holy habitation, which, being placed in the center of the world, sees all things that partake of generations. And when he had called them together he spake as follows: Here it ends.

APPENDIX TWO

TIMAEUS

TIMAEUS IS ONE OF THE dialogs written by Plato around 360 BCE. It is important because it is one of the two earliest references to Atlantis in world literature.

Timaeus is a dialog in which Critias, Plato's great-grandfather, describes the origin of the world to Socrates. It contains an introduction to Atlantis and description of its destruction. The translation that appears below is from *Atlantis: The Antediluvian World* by Ignatius Donnelly (New York: Harper & Brothers, 1882).

> **Critias:** Then listen, Socrates, to a strange tale, which is, however, certainly true, as Solon, who was the wisest of the seven sages, declared. He was a relative and great friend of my great grandfather, Dropidas, as he himself says in several of his poems; and Dropidas told Critias, my grandfather, who remembered and told us that there were of old great and marvelous actions of the Athenians, which have passed into oblivion through time and the destruction of the human race—and one in particular—which

was the greatest of them all, the recital of which will be a suitable testimony of our gratitude to you . . .

Socrates: Very good, and what is this ancient famous action of which Critias spoke, not as mere legend, but as a veritable action of the Athenian state, which Solon recounted?

Critias: I will tell an old-world story, which I heard from an aged man; for Critias was, as he said, at that time nearly ninety years of age, and I was about ten years of age. Now the day was that day, the third of the festival of the Apaturia, which is called the registration of youth; at which, according to custom, our parents gave prizes for recitations, and the poems of several poets were recited by us boys, and many of us sang the poems of Solon, which were new at the time. One of our tribe, either because this was his real opinion or because he thought that he would please Critias, said that in his judgment Solon was not only the wisest of men but the noblest of poets. The old, I well remember, brightened at this and said, smiling: "Yes, Amynander, if Solon had only, like other poets, made poetry the business of his life and had completed the tale he brought with him from Egypt, and had not been compelled, by reason of the factions and troubles he found stirring in this country when he came home, to attend to other matters, in my opinion he would have been as famous as Homer or Hesiod or any poets."

"And what was that poem about, Critias?" said the person who addressed him.

"About the greatest action the Athenians ever did, and which ought to have been most famous, but which, through the lapse of time and the destruction of the actors, has not come down to us."

"Tell us," said the other, "the whole story, and how and from whom Solon heard this veritable tradition."

He replied: "At the head of the Egyptian delta, where the river Nile divides, there is a certain district called the district of Sais, and the great city of the district is also called Sais, and is the city from which sprang Amasis the king. And the citizens have a deity who is their foundress: she is called in the Egyptian tongue Neith, which is asserted by them to be the same whom the Greeks called Athene. Now the citizens of this city are great lovers of the Athenians, and say that they are in some way related to them. Thither came Solon, who was received by them with great honor; and he asked the priests, who were most skillful in such matters, about antiquity, and made the discovery that neither he nor any other Greek knew anything worth mentioning about the times of old. On one occasion, when he was drawing [on] them to speak of antiquity, he began to tell about the most ancient things in our part of the world about Phonroneus, who is called "the first," and about Niobe, and after the deluge, to tell of the lives of Deucalion and Pyrrha, and he traced the genealogy of their descendants and attempted to reckon how many years old were the events of which he was speaking, and to give the dates."

Whereupon one of the priests who was of very great age said "O Solon, Solon, you Greeks are but children, and there is never an old man who is a Greek." Solon, hearing this, said, "What do you mean?" "I mean to say," he replied, "that in mind you are all young; there is no old opinion handed down among you by ancient tradition, nor any science that is hoary with age. And I will tell you the reason of this: There have been, and there will be again, many destructions of mankind out of many causes. There is a story that even you have preserved, that once upon a time Phaethon, the son of Helios, having yoked the steeds in his father's chariot because he was not able to drive them in the path of his father, burnt up all that was upon the earth, and was himself destroyed by a thunderbolt. Now, this has the form of a myth but really signifies a deviation from their courses of the bodies moving around the earth and in the heavens, a great conflagration of things upon the earth recurring at long intervals of time. When this happens, those who live upon the mountains and in dry and lofty places are more liable to destruction than those who dwell by rivers or on the seashore; and from this calamity the fact that we live on the low-lying land by the Nile, who is our never-failing savior, saves and delivers us. When, on the other hand, the gods purge the earth with a deluge of water, among your herdsmen and shepherds on the mountains are the survivors; whereas those of you who live in the cities are swept by the waters into the sea. But in this country neither at that time nor at any other does the water come from above on the fields, having always a tendency to come up from below, for which reason the things preserved here are said to be the oldest. The fact is that wherever the extremity of winter frost or summer sun does not prevent, the human race is always increasing at times, and at other times diminishing in numbers. And whatever happened either in your country or in ours, or in any other region of which we are informed, if any action that is noble or great or in any other way remarkable has taken; whereas you and other nations, having just provided yourselves with letters and the other things that states require, and when the stream from heaven descends like a pestilence and leaves only those of you who are destitute of letters and education; and thus you have to begin all over again as children, and know nothing of what happened in ancient times, either among us or among yourselves. As for your genealogies recounted to us, Solon, they are no better than the tales of children; for in the first place, you remember one deluge only, whereas there were many before that; and, in the next, you do not know that there dwelt in your land the fairest and noblest race of men that ever lived, of whom you and your whole city are but a seed or remnant. And this was unknown to you because for many generations the survivors of that destruction died and made no sign. For there was a time, Solon, before that great deluge of all, when the city that is now Athens was first in war and was preeminent for the excellence of her laws, and is said to have performed the noblest of deeds, and to have had the fairest constitution of any of which tradition tell, under the face of heaven." Solon marveled at this and earnestly requested the priest to inform him exactly and in order about these former citizens. "You are welcome to hear about them," said the priest "both for your own sake and for that of the city; and above all, for the sake of the goddess who is the common mother and protector and educator of both our cities. She founded your city a thousand years before ours, when Gaea and Hephaestus established your race; and then she founded ours, the constitution of which is set down in our sacred registers as eight thousand years old. As touching the citizens of nine thousand years ago, I will briefly inform you of their laws and of the noblest of their actions; and the exact particulars of the whole we will hereafter go through at our leisure in the sacred registers themselves. If you compare these very laws with your own you will find that many of ours are the counterpart of yours, as they were in olden time. In the first place, there is the caste of priests, which is separate from all others; next there are the artificers, who exercise their several crafts by themselves and without admixture of any other; and also there is the class of shepherds and that of hunters, as well as that of husbandmen; and you will observe, too, that the warriors in Egypt are separated from all the other classes and are commanded by the law only to engage in war; moreover, the weapons with which they are equipped are shields and spears, and this the goddess taught first among you and then in Asiatic countries, and we among the Asiatics first adopted.

Then as to wisdom, do you observe what care the law took from the very first, searching out and comprehending [the] whole order of things down to prophecy and medicine, the latter with a view to health? And out of these divine elements drawing what was needful for human life, and adding every sort of knowledge that was connected with them. All this order and arrangement the goddess first imparted to you when establishing your city; and she chose the spot of earth in which you were born because she saw that the happy temperament of the seasons in that land would produce the wisest of men. Wherefore the goddess, who was a lover both of war and of wisdom, selected, and first of all settled that spot that was most likely to produce men likest herself. And there you dwelt, having such laws as these and still better ones, and excelled all mankind in all virtue, as became the children and disciples of the gods. Many great and wonderful deeds are recorded of your state in our histories, but one of them exceeds all the rest in greatness and valor; for these histories tell of a mighty power that was aggressing wantonly against the whole of Europe and Asia, and to which your city put an end. This power had landed on the Atlantic coast, for in those days the Atlantic was navigable from an island situated to the west of the straits, called the Pillars of Hercules. The island was larger than Libya and Asia put together, and from it could be reached other islands, and from the islands you might pass through to the opposite continent (the Americas), which surrounded the true ocean; for this sea, which is within the Columns of Hercules, is only a harbor, having a narrow entrance; but that other is a real sea, and the surrounding land may be most truly called a continent. Now, the island was called Atlantis and was the heart of a great and wonderful empire that had rule over the whole island and several others, as well as over parts of the continent; and, besides these, parts of Libya as far as Egypt, and of Europe as far as Tyrrhenia. The vast power thus gathered into one endeavored to subdue at one blow our country and yours, and the whole of the land that was within the straits; and then, Solon, your country shone forth in the excellence of her virtue and strength among all mankind; for she was the first in courage and military skill, and was the leader of the Hellenic allies. And when the rest fell from her, being compelled to stand alone after having undergone the very extremity of danger, she defeated and triumphed over the invaders and preserved from slavery and freely liberated all the others who were not yet subjected, and freely liberated all the others who dwelt within the limits of Heracles. But afterward there occurred violent earthquakes and floods, and in a single day and night of rain, all your warlike men in a body sank into the earth, and the island of Atlantis in like manner disappeared beneath the sea. And that is the reason why the sea in those parts is impassable and impenetrable, because there is such a great quantity of impassible mud.

APPENDIX THREE

A DEEPER LOOK AT THE CRESPI COLLECTION OF CUENCA, ECUADOR

By Warren Cook and Warren Dexter

Reprinted from an article that appeared in Midwestern Epigraphic Journal *Volume 17, November 2, 2003, pp. 23–37, by kind permission of Beverly Moseley, publisher.*

Weakened by acute bronchopneumonia, Padre Carlo Crespi's valiant heart stopped on the evening of April 30, 1982, one month short of his reaching ninety. As the old priest's memory dimmed in his last years, so did hope of learning the details of provenance of some of the most remarkable artifacts ever turned up in the Americas.

I first heard of the Crespi Collection from Professor Barry Fell, an expert in ancient Middle Eastern languages, who showed me a slide taken in Cuenca in 1978 by Brigham Young University historian Dr.

Paul Cheesman of what has come to be called the "Masinissa Plaque." The plaque had been projected and briefly interpreted by Fell during his evening address at the "Ancient Vermont" conference at Castleton State College in 1977, and portions of it were pictured and discussed in his book *Saga America: A Startling New Theory on the Old World Settlement of America before Columbus*, first published in 1980.

The gold-colored, roller-stamped, rectangular metal plaque with a perfectly round hole cut from its center announces the death of Masinissa (King of the Libyan-Egyptians, known to have died in 148 BCE) and the ascension of his son to the throne of a united Egypt.

A gold-like plaque from the same collection on another Cheesman slide bears the image of a bird with outstretched wings, and beneath it, two bearded, hooded, clergy-like men carrying staffs. On either side, in grid panels of script, Fell pointed out letters in a variation of Cypriot, spelling "Ku-kul-ka-na" and "Ko-et-tse-tse-ve-ko-atl," telling of a mission to a land called "sunset" and discovery of *tla-o-lee* (the Aztec word for maize). I recognized the correspondence to the Mayan Kukulkan and Aztecan Quetzalcoatl, alleged white-skinned, bearded Central American deities or culture heroes. But both names on a single plaque, and from South America!

John Cole, then instructor in anthropology at Hartwick College in Oneonta, New York, immediately assailed Fell from the floor of the conference for using artifacts from the collection of a man "who is relatively well-known in Ecuador as somebody who is very confused about what he collects, and has spread the word that he will buy anything if it looks impressive.

Subsequently, Cheesman showed me [Warren Cook] additional photos he had taken of Crespi relics that obviously did not fit into the known parameters of Andean archaeology. Since Cuenca, anciently called Tomebamba (Tumi-Pampa), or "plain of the knife" in Quechua, language of the Incas, functioned as northern capital of the Inca Empire under three monarchs, it is not an unlikely place for antiquities treasured from past millennia to surface. Because my [anthropologist Warren Cook's] specialty is Andean culture history and I have been researching Incan religion since 1947, I felt a responsibility to see the Crespi collection for myself and have its significant components adequately photographed in color by Warren W. Dexter.

Given the difficulties inherent in photographing and studying the Crespi Collection, as well as my Andean experience and linguistic advantage, Cheesman and I drew up a plan of action: a between-semesters, three-week visit to Cuenca accompanied by Dexter. [Professor] Cheesman would meet us in Cuenca. Another Ancient Vermont conference attendee, Charles Hepburn, had a Pennsylvania friend (Donald Rasmussen) with a contact in Cuenca (Alfonso Serrano), from whom he was able to learn up-to-date details about the state of the aged Padre's precarious health and the collection's current accessibility.

In late December of 1977, Warren and I [Cheesman] had reservations to Guayaquil when a call came from Hepburn, who warned us that because of his increased frailty, Crespi no longer had a key to the rooms with the most important portion of his collection. The call from Serrano to Rasmussen to Hepburn to Cook aborted our trip—and saved Cheesman's life, in that Paul canceled his own reservation on a flight from Guayaquil to Cuenca, which, as it turned out, crashed against an Andean mountaintop, killing all on board.

In the months that followed, reports from Cuenca did not improve prospects of access to the controversial assemblage. Word came in 1979 that the old man was at death's door, and the collection in peril of dispersal. The urgency of recording on color film anything that remained became even more imperative. Eventually, knowing only that Padre Crespi was reportedly still alive, Warren Dexter and I arrived in Guayaquil on June 15, 1981.

Four hours of fearful careening in a speedy *fulgoneta,* a van whose driver seemed more like a pilot flying low, brought us up through the clouds, over the Continental Divide, and down into the exquisite valley of Cuenca.

The city of Cuenca lies on a tributary of the Amazon in a fertile basin high in the Andes. It is the bustling capital of Azuay province, and not far from its center is a flat-topped hill called Puma Pongo (Puma gate), reputed to be the site of the palace of Tupac Inca Yupanqui, the tenth Sapa Inca, or Incan ruler, who added southern Ecuador to Tawantinsuyu (Empire of the Four Corners of the World). His son, Huayna Capac, and grandson, Atahualpa, were born there. At 2,576 meters (about 8,000 feet), Cuenca is sufficiently high that breathing deeply is a constant task for the unaccustomed.

Our modest hotel was less than a block from the Museo del Banco Central, the provincial museum owned and administered by the Ecuadorian Treasury Department's Central Bank. As we soon learned, the Banco Central had purchased the Crespi Collection, and everything deemed worthwhile had been transferred to its local museum, where Director Licenciado Rene Cardozo and his helpful staff extended us every possible assistance.

The evening of our arrival, Alfonso Serrano was ill, but the very next day his wife took us to meet Padre Crespi. We found him readily in the confessional bearing his nameplate, just to the right inside the Church of Maria Auxiliadora's front entrance. The ninety-year-old priest greeted us eagerly in heavily Italian-accented Spanish, breaking away from a dozen men and women of every age and social class who clustered around him. As we went out to the sidewalk, he seized me by the lapel and rambled on about things crowding his mind, all the while acceding to a constant stream of people who came up, knelt, and kissed his hand saying, "Dame su bendicion, santo Padre." (Give me your blessing, saintly Father.)

Señora Serrano had introduced me as a North American professor who had come to study his collection, to which he responded vehemently: "Ay, eso me lo han robado todo"! (Ay, they have robbed me of all that!) Not once in the ensuing fifteen minutes did I succeed in turning the conversation to anything pertinent to his collection. The kindly old man had a warm sparkle in his eyes—obviously he enjoyed foreign visitors—and was robust of voice, but it was evident that arteriosclerosis had robbed us of the chance to learn anything relevant from him.

Later that day, Richard Boroto, director of the binational Centro Cultural Abraham Lincoln, acquainted us with which way the bull "went through the pea patch," so far as local authorities were concerned. Searching out these savants, we soon pieced together a pathetic picture for New World history. Some of its nuances may never be clarified, even for those closest to the scene. But knowledge of these circumstances is crucial to evaluating the significance of the collection's anomalous items.

Carlo Crespi Croci was born in Legnano, near Milan, Italy, on May 29, 1891, but not into a family of dukes, as some have said. His father, Daniel, a farm administrator, opposed the boy's priestly vocation, but his mother, Luisa, was supportive. Third among thirteen children, at age five he began to assist a local priest. In Milan and Turin he attended schools run by the Salesians, an order founded in 1856 by John Bosco to care for poor and needy teenagers, using a system of education based on reason, religion, and kindness. Those values that the Salesians imbued are key to understanding the course of young Carlo's subsequent concerns.

At fifteen he became a novice in Foglizzo (Turin), and was ordained in Verona at twenty-six. Four years of study at the secular University of Padua with a thesis in anthropology gave him a master's degree. A dissertation about a previously unknown aspect of Paduan fauna earned him a doctorate in natural sciences in 1921. He then obtained doctorates at the same university in music and engineering. All of these would be evident in his subsequent achievements.

Crespi came to Ecuador for the first time in 1923, not as a missionary, but to gather scientific data and artifacts for an international missions exhibition to be held in Rome in 1925 and 1926, material he subsequently exhibited in New York City in 1928 through 1929.

Returning to Ecuador in 1926 and again in 1931, Crespi was assigned to a Salesian mission at Macas in Ecuador's Oriente, or Amazon region. His jungle stint was brief, and the following year he returned permanently to Cuenca. In 1933 he commenced the five-year labor of constructing the Instituto Cornelio Merchan, an imposing four-storied boys elementary and trade school. He became its first director.

Crespi told a journalist that his impulse to create a museum came from having encountered an ancient potsherd during excavations for the foundation of Cornelio Merchan. The same interviewer then asked: "Is it certain that, Padre Crespi, has been sold things that have no scientific value? That they swindle you?" To these questions he answered: *"En soma, permitame. Esto no lo ponga. Todavia hay in Cuenca, hay muchos que tienen hambrey, el P. Crespi lo sabe . . ."* (In summary: permit me. Don't put that down. In Cuenca there are still many people who experience hunger, and Padre Crespi knows it . . .)

"When my father passed away in Italy," Crespi once told a compatriot, "he left me a legacy, and I could think of no better way to use it than by salvaging their ancient treasures from the greedy traders and black marketers."

While serving at Macas, Crespi had filmed *Los Terribles Shuara de Alto Amazonas* (The Terrible Jivaros of the Upper Amazon). As an educator he was devoted to the use of motion pictures, importing some forty of them. He loved to explain beforehand what his charges were expected to perceive. Woe betide the boy who fell short of the Padre's expectations. Watching over them with a [hand] bell, he didn't hesitate to rap on the head of any lad who didn't behave appropriately.

Carlo Crespi had a passion for learning and creativity. His former secretary, Imbabura-born Padre Luis Flores-Haro (who began serving in Cuenca in 1951), tells how Crespi over and over again repeated, *"Siempre quise que mis ninos comprendan bien las cosas."* (I always wanted my boys to understand things well.) Crespi published numerous musical works of his own composition and formed the best band in Ecuador; several of its members are currently illustrious components of the Musical

Conservatory of Cuenca. He is credited with introducing skill mastery into Cuenca's primary education. He founded the Agricultural School (in 1931) in Yanuncay, a Cuenca suburb, and nearby by the Instituto Orientalista of Cuenca (1940), which prepares young men for ministry in the Amazon region.

On average, Crespi had to worry about feeding two thousand students daily. He also assisted countless mothers with children who came to him each day seeking means to survive, a practice that we observed [Father Crespi's student and friend] Padre Flores-Haro still maintained.

In 1962, Colegio Cornelio Merchan [where Padre Crespi kept his collection] burned to the ground. Although a room holding some of the best of the collection was destroyed, the majority was spared in the old wing that remains today. On the ruined site, Crespi and his brethren in time erected the present church of Maria Auxiliadora.

Padre Crespi never lacked local recognition for his accomplishments; Ecuador awarded him a medal in 1935, and that same year the Ministry of Education gave him another medal. In 1974 a street was named after him, as the new school being built with funds from the sale of his collection to the Museo de Banco Central. In January of 1982, scant months before his death, Italy conferred on him the Medal of Merit of the Republic and Cuenca again declared him its adoptive son.

Crespi's kind deeds over the decades earned the nonagenarian a secure place in the hearts of people of all classes. It is legend that it was never too late to knock on the street-level window of the Padre's quarters to ask him to go out and administer last rites to someone in his parish. His bedroom was close to the courtyard door, and the relatives of the sick and dying came to get him when someone needed the sacrament of Extreme Unction for the dying. *"Yo voy!"* (I'm going) he would always answer, and moments later be underway, it having been his habit to retire dressed, lying on newspapers spread out over his bed.

A taxi driver, hearing us discuss him, volunteered that "every family in Cuenca will want to accompany him to his grave." Dr. Ezequiel

Clavijo, an archaeologist and legislator from Cuenca, told me, "All Cuenca will overflow with tears the day that Padre Crespi dies. One time I was with him when a woman approached with an obviously bogus object for sale, and he pulled several coins out of his cassock and bought it. When I told him it lacked any value, he said, 'I know it, but they don't have any other means of living.'" A similar incident was reported by Dr. Carlos Ramirez Salcedo of the University of Cuenca, one of Ecuador's most respected archaeologists.

It was the Padre's charitable penchant for buying anything and everything offered to him that led to the fate that has befallen the collection. Apologists say he wanted to keep sources of valuable relics from drying up. Flores told me Crespi frequently said his purchase of potentially idolatrous objects stemmed from a concern "that the people not have them in their houses, and thus I liberate them from fetishism." According to Flores, countless small amulets were acquired over the years, but all had now been disposed of, "where they will never be found," he informed me zealously.

Flores-Haro tells how Crespi, long after his priestly labors were finished, would stay awake three or four more hours reading history and archaeology. From such study, and from the Egyptian, Babylonian, and Phoenician appearance of some of the objects in the collection, decades ago Crespi arrived at the conviction that there had been ancient Mediterranean contacts with Ecuador. The more his views met resistance, the more dogmatic he became on the subject when guiding visitors through his collection.

The consensus opinion of Ecuadorian archaeologists was that Cuencan artisans, always noted for their skill and inventiveness, began to bring the Padre objects particularly crafted to suit his predilection. Many tons of sculpted stones, great piles of embossed metal sheets, thirteen hundred paintings, numerous polychrome statues, and countless pieces of pottery, whole and in shards, obstructed school operations by clogging rooms, lining balconies, and littering courtyards.

Obvious to everyone, even to Crespi himself, much of his trove was of recent fabrication. Matters worsened when Erich von Däniken's book *The Gold of the Gods* (1972) alleged that Crespi's strangest relics came from an extensive network of tunnels stacked with two to three thousand metal plates bearing ancient inscriptions, in the province of Morona-Santiago, not far east of Cuenca but difficult to access. Juan Moricz, a Hungarian and naturalized Argentinean, allegedly had stumbled upon them in 1965, and von Däniken claimed to have been taken there in 1972. Following publication of *The Gold of the Gods,* Flores says, so many foreigners visited Maria Auxiliadora to see Padre Crespi that it became something of a nuisance.

Subsequently, a government-backed expedition failed to find anything of importance in the Cueva de los Tayos, the suspected site. I talked with Cuencan archaeologist Juan Cordero Yniguez, who had been to los Tayos and saw nothing to warrant giving the bird-dung littered cavern any further attention. Others claim that Moricz, who in 1981 still lived in Zamora, had never disclosed the actual cave in question. But official disappointment blighted local enthusiasm, and in Cuenca, von Däniken is regarded as a liar and fantasist.

In March of 1979, Crespi was struck low by illness, received the last rites, and for a time lay near death. The old man's constitution was strong, however, and a prostate operation eventually put him back on his feet. Nonetheless, a decision was made while he was helpless, and in January of 1980, implementation commenced. For 13,000,000 sucres ($433,000), the Museo del Banco Central purchased the Crespi Collection with an option to select or reject as its experts saw fit. With the proceeds the Salesians are now constructing a new school, appropriately named in his honor. But the money is already exhausted, according to Padre Flores-Haro, and $200,000 will be needed to finish the basic physical plant. Carlo Crespi school will readily accommodate the 640 boys now in primary grades, but an additional $66,000 would be needed to build a second story over one wing for a gallery to display appropriately what remains of the priest's collection.

When the process of selection began in February of 1980, as best could be managed the old priest was shielded from seeing his "treasures" removed, but at times "se puso bravo"—he went into a rage. Sorting had to take place behind locked doors to keep him from interrupting. Dust hung thick in the air as ceiling-high tiers of Inca jars, metal-sheathed statues, and embossed plaques were lowered to the floor. Participants in this labor claim they still cannot shake off respiratory ailments dating from the experience.

Specialists were appointed to separate the wheat from the chaff: Dr. Gustavo Reinosa Hermidia of Cuenca, and Dr. Olaf Holm, Director of the Museo del Banco Central of Guayaquil, were the archaeologists charged with sorting ceramics and stone respectively. About one-third of the ceramics proved valuable, by Reinoso's estimate. They range over every Ecuadorian period but the earliest—Valdivia—and include hundreds of truly superb examples. Some 8,000 pieces plus countless shards were transferred to the Museo for cataloging, storage, and eventual exhibition. About 1,300 paintings—ninth-century to colonial—were removed to the same repository, as well as numerous old polychrome religious statues of all sizes, all from the Crespi Collection.

Except for about eight giant stone seats from Mante, a few headrests, and perhaps a dozen other stunning pieces, the balance of the lithic material—many, many tons—was judged worthless. In this all local authorities seem to have concurred, since uncounted hundreds of stones were dispensed with from congested corridors and potential classrooms. The Salesians opted to give them to any and all takers. Dr. Reinoso told me that on one occasion, upon entering a patio he saw fresh cement being poured over an area filled in with carved stones. The hundreds of rejected embossed metal plates and three-dimensional metallic objects were moved up to the old school's fourth-floor attic.

This was the situation our photographer, Warren Dexter, and I encountered upon arriving in Cuenca. Seeing the superb pre-Columbian pottery, valuable paintings, polychrome sculpture, and the few remarkable stones in the Museo del Banco Central immediately increased our respect for Crespi as a collector and preserver of art. Reportedly, nothing had been taken to Quito. Museum authorities had no knowledge of the whereabouts of the other stone, metal, or ceramic objects left behind, and welcomed our investigative efforts, collaborating in every way.

Through the museum we were introduced to Padre Flores-Haro on June 22 and were escorted to the fourth-floor attic, where the remnants of metal objects and ceramics left by the Banco Central's experts were scattered in total disarray. Dexter was allowed time for only a few overall pictures, which, when later printed, would show a number of significant pieces that had escaped our notice under such hasty circumstances. Then, from his own quarters Flores-Haro brought down into the courtyard three of the objects, which he said Crespi had treasured the most:

1. A zodiac plate with a grid of fifty-six symbols embossed on a 51- by 13-inch oblong sheet of remarkably unoxidized copper alloy, which Fell considers Paphian script accompanying the corresponding zodiac signs.
2. A rectangular pyramid plaque embossed on the same type of burnished alloy and bearing a panel of lettering across the pyramid's base that Fell identifies as neo-Punic Phoenician script, but which translates meaningfully in Quechua, a dialect of Ecuador.
3. A large brownish-black ceramic jar bearing symbols identified by Fell as Cypriot, but translating meaningfully in Quechua.

As for the hundreds of stones given away, no records had been kept, but Flores-Haro recalled some of the destinations:

1. Cuenca's Cuartel Cayambe, a closely guarded army base
2. The impressive new multimillion-dollar Artipracticas furniture manufacturing plant at Zuchay, not far south of Cuenca
3. Colegio Agronomica Salesiana

4. Colegio Orientalist Salesiano in Yanuncay, a suburb south of Cuenca
5. Colegio Nacional Kleber Franco Cruz in far-off Machala, near the Peruvian border (whence a big truckload had been taken when two science teachers there, former Crespi students, learned that they were being given away

Enumerating this list is easy in hindsight, but extracting it from informants, finding, gaining access, and photographing the stones thus located involved weeks of inordinate detective work, diplomacy, and travel. There was even a wild goose chase involving twenty-one hours in a bus on an incredibly tortuous, bumpy, and muddy road over three successive Andean ranges to a nonexistent Colegio San Juan Bautista in Loja. With much assistance from a number of very kind people, we ascertained there is no likelihood that any of the schools in Loja have any of the Crespi stones, and that particular trail is cold.

The other reputed destinations, however, all paid off. Once into zealously guarded Cayambe we found forty or so large sculptures, many of them monstrous in their demonic conception. Discounting several obviously modern confections of wood, cement, and plaster of paris, most of the remainder in their ugly but vigorous force suggest idols described in Jose de Arriaga's *Extirpation de la Idolatria* (Lima, 1611), which describes a time when priests in Peru were dismayed to find such statues secretly built into Christian chapels or hidden deep within underground chambers where they were still receiving shamanistic cult worship. Upon consulting stone sculptors at work near Cuenca, we learned that similar-size carvings would require a minimum of three weeks apiece for one artisan to complete. Each is a unique, albeit grotesque, artistic creation of a vivid imagination.

The owner of the Artepracticas factory at Zuchay, reportedly one of the wealthiest individuals in Ecuador, had selected for an intended exhibit a particularly interesting group of large, flat stones bearing rectangular grid patterns, each square containing characters similar to those on metal plaques and headpieces we were unable to locate, but which had been translated by Fell from Cheesman photographs. Stones from the Crespi Collection doubtless migrated elsewhere in the diaspora of 1980 and may turn up in due time, particularly if there is local publicity as to their potential importance.

There was less interest in removing from Maria Auxiliadora the school's embarrassment of metallic objects. Several huge plaques, recognizably bogus, had been used to sheath a kiosk. With the exception of a few metal plaques at the Colegio Agronomico, the rest that we saw were in the fourth-floor attic, to which Warren and I were admitted a second time on the eve of our departure, and then only in response to my plea of despair at departing without having had further opportunity to assess the accumulation.

In one attic room we found a score of bronze castings, some of them recognizable from Cheesman photos, which Fell suggested were ancient Phoenician-Cypriot copies of religious and historical motifs of various earlier Middle Eastern civilizations, fabricated as trade gifts with overseas customers. One may depict Cleopatra, bitten in the breast by an asp (implying a date post 30 BCE); another may be David carrying Goliath's severed head (a dent on the monstrous brow supports such an interpretation). One portrays a Syrian bird-headed genie (Nisroch) and the Tree of Life. Accompanying the bronze plaques, cast by the lost wax process, are several rough castings of the same motifs. From their pitted surfaces and imperfections, as well as the fusing of motifs from several distinct cultures, I suspect them to be of local artisanship, showing the difficulty of emulating such a complicated technique without firsthand instruction, guided solely by observing the imports.

From the dust-covered objects littering the floor of one room, Padre Flores-Haro lifted a small hoop that he particularly treasured, the emerald- and gold-encrusted crown from the image of Maria Auxiliadora, so damaged by the fire of 1962 that only the Padre's personal memory would have distinguished it from the other clutter.

We saw the fantastic metal-sheathed statues described by Hugh Fox and Pino Turolla: the man in armor with modern false teeth and a curved-tail beast, for which, Flores-Haro assured me sorrowfully, Crespi paid the equivalent of five thousand dollars—yet obviously worthless. Flores-Haro named the fabricator, a still living Azuay artisan.

Crespi had shown compatriot Pino Turolla a drawer full of paintings that the friar claimed were by Old Masters: Leonardo, Rafael, Cimabue, Botticelli, and Tintoretto—forty or fifty of them, and for all Turolla could tell, they were genuine. When asked how they came to be in his possession, Crespi responded: "My order is one of the oldest in Italy. Many of our founders were sons of great Italian families—families that go back to the Renaissance and before. Their families had these paintings. But times were very troubled in Italy then, and they were gathered together by our order and brought here for safekeeping."

Italian-born Padre Virgilio Berassi of the Instituto Orientalista Salesiano of Cuenca, when asked about this, told me he never saw any Old Masters, but Crespi was fond of making such wild claims and never let visitors get very close to any of his treasures. Crespi called many of the metal pieces "gold" and brought them out one at a time, but never let anyone else so much as heft them. Numerous objects photographed by foreigners and alleged to be gold turned out, upon our inspection, to be of burnished—presumably copper—alloy. These contrasted notably, however, with the very tarnished surface of crudely designed pieces, some of which bore, upon the reverse side and in English, the modern manufacturer's annealed trademark.

One famous artist represented in the Crespi collection was Francisco de Goya, by a tapestry woven in Madrid from one of his early paintings; the Museo values it at ten thousand dollars. The Crespi canvases, with few exceptions, seem to have been painted in America by little-known artists, albeit often of considerable quality. In the 1960s he had been officially prevented from shipping a collection of colonial canvasses to Italy, presumably for sale to support his beloved school. Expertly restored, they are now the pride of Cuenca's Casa de Cultura.

No charges were brought against the Padre, and our inquiries disclosed that prior to the incident the government's attitude toward protecting such things was not as sensitive as it is now, and unrestored old paintings often were purchased and taken abroad without hindrance.

The old friar had a standard spiel. Visitors would hear how one of the pharaohs had left Egypt and traveled up the Amazon to settle in southern Ecuador. Inquiring around, Turolla was told that Crespi had collected "books and pictures of Egyptian, Phoenician, and other Old World cultures, given them to the natives, and said: 'If you ever find anything like this, bring it to me and I will reward you.'" The Father Superior in Cuenca, Pedro Lova, confessed to Turolla that Crespi's "voluminous and ever-growing collection, and his strange ideas, were an embarrassment both to him and to the order." From the vast quantity of obviously bogus items, Turolla concluded that Crespi "was living in a dreamworld of his own creation." Cuencan authorities, prior to our visit, were convinced that Crespi's anomalous objects most likely were copied from illustrations from foreign sources. But since Turolla's time, local esteem for the quality of much of the material in his collection had vastly improved. That many authentic Andean treasures were mingled with the dross is testified by the superb selection now in possession of the Museo del Banco Central, for which the government was willing to pay $433,000.

Fox, Turolla, and previous Cuencan opinion notwithstanding, some of Crespi's unique relics should be considered authentically ancient on the basis of internal evidence. Who in Ecuador would be capable of counterfeiting inscriptions in Cypriot or Phoenician, for which no published sources are known to exist? That the Padre obtained them from Europe is improbable, considering that some of them translate in Quechua. The many large slabs at Zuchay bearing recognizable Cypriot letters within grids are so heavy as to discount the modern import theory. The inference is that at sometime past, Andean artisans had access to knowledge of a variety of Mediterranean scripts.

It would appear that first-millennium BCE navigators had trade contact with native sovereigns of the Cuenca region, their likely objective being the abundant gold in that area. The date of the Masinissa Plaque, 148 BCE, corresponds archaeologically with a handsomely decorated Ecuadorian ceramic type called Cero Narrio, about whose culture and political structure little is known, since it long preceded Canari and Inca traditions.

On the last day of the time we had available for research in Cuenca, the Masinissa Plaque still had not come to light. Padre Flores-Haro did not recall ever seeing it, but both Dr. Gustavo Reinosa and Dr. Benigno Malo, editors of the *Revista de Anthropologia,* remember commenting upon its Egyptian quality, although they considered it completely anachronistic, and all the metal sheets "only worth melting down." Now, on the eve of our departure, with Padre Flores-Haro's blessing, Reinoso was enthusiastic about rummaging through the fourth-floor attic in search of the plaque. If it was still there, he was certain he could find it.

In Quito we showed our color prints from the Crespi Collections to architect Hernan Crespo Toral, nationwide director of the museums of the Banco Central. He, too, remembered having seen the Masinissa Plaque—the size and shape, with its hole, of a three- by five-inch back of a rounded desk blotter. Although it is unique, he felt certain that many similar had been manufactured as gifts for Cuenca's doctors earlier in the present century, and one ended up among Crespi's artifacts. As to how it could bear three types of exotic yet translatable script, he showed no real concern, falling back upon the assurances of his authorities that all of Crespi's objects not selected for the museum were of recent fabrication.

One scholar's modern ink blotter holder is another's trilingual proclamation of stunning historical import! And then the artifact itself gets lost! Both men have integrity. Wherein lies the truth? Without informing him of the importance of his answer, I called Paul Cheesman upon returning to Vermont and asked him to recall the size of the Masinissa

Plaque. His response: it was approximately four by eight inches in size, with a one-and-a-half inch hole. Cheesman's understanding was that Crespi knew the name of the man on whose farm it had been found; that he had it made into an ink blotter holder, and upon the man's death it had come into the Padre's possession.

Nor could we locate the elephant stela photographed by J. Manson Valentine and published by Charles Berlitz (1972). Crespi had said it was found during construction of Cuenca's airport. It bore Libyan script of the finest style, which translates as, "The elephant that supports the earth and therefore is the cause of the earthquake." That it once existed is beyond doubt, and that anyone in Ecuador could have counterfeited it stretches credulity.

To some extent, dismemberment of the Crespi Collection stems from the zealous Padre's conduct. He was eager to have foreign investigators take pictures, but seldom brought out the same important piece twice. Because of the bogus items, professional archaeologists paid him no attention. Judging from his cagey treatment of our predecessors, had we arrived in 1978 as originally planned, we probably would have fared no better. In 1981 Padre Flores permitted us to take careful color photographs, albeit during very limited time. We were too late to see some of Crespi's other significant artifacts, which may be lost forever.

It would appear that many years ago Crespi concluded that his favorite pieces were genuine and of ancient Mediterranean derivation, yet disinterred locally. A man of impressive learning, he realized that his treasures reflected some kind of contact with the Old World. Convinced of this, deservedly so, and with the prospect that more evidence ought to be forthcoming, he began the practice of indiscriminate collecting in the belief that it kept his sources flowing and truly served his parishioners, while relieving them of objects he judged idolatrous.

His foxy-clever behavior tantalized foreign scholars, but prevented close inspection of what was worthwhile. As a consequence, everyone began to doubt his judgment. Before the aged priest was willing to give up his mortal shell, illness pried loose his grasp upon the incredible accumulation. Only that which fit the present consensus paradigm of Andean cultural history was taken into government custody. Much of the rest was scattered to the wind.

Day after day, the owner and employees of Cuenca's Foto Ortiz graciously interrupted their normal, busy routine to develop Warren Dexter's photographs within a few hours time, which greatly assisted me in demonstrating to Ecuadorian scientists that portions of the collection left behind by the Museo del Banco Central or scattered far and wide merited protecting until further studied. His color prints raised the level of awareness of the issue among local savants, and became a factor in their evolving perception of Ecuador's remote past.

Padre Flores-Haro's plan for a gallery at the new school to display the Crespi relics that remain in Salesian hands is worthy. Hopefully it will find the monetary support it merits, but Flores-Haro was subsequently named director of the Don Bosco school in far-off Quito, where he took up residence in August 1982, thus further weakening the link between the anomalous artifacts and their past.

The Museo del Banco Central plans to excavate Puma Pongo, site of the Inca palace in Cuenca, and construct a museum there to store, study, and display what it purchased from the Salesians. Such a dig, if thorough, would be very valuable. The ideal physical location of Tomebamba was appreciated by Inca monarchs, and excavation there promises to disclose much about their predecessors, who presumably would have taken advantage of the prominent hill as well.

Crespi was not the first to acquire metal artifacts in Cuenca of the exotic style in question, as shown by a BBC program screened on American Educational TV in the spring of 1981, *Treasures of Buckingham Palace,* which included a supposedly gold crown very similar in aspect to a Crespi example. The Lord Chamberlain's office confirms that it was the gift of President Gabriel Garcia Moreno in 1854, and reportedly excavated in Cuenca. A single comparable artifact found tomorrow in an archaeological contest could vindicate Carlo Crespi's perceptiveness, if not his judgment.

That the old Padre had acquired some of the most anachronistic objects in New World archaeology is evident. That they were disinterred in or near Cuenca—ancient Tomebamba—seems very likely. Whether still available or known only through photographs, they have cracked open a bit wider a door that was slammed shut when Rome destroyed Carthage and then subjugated the Libyan-Egyptians, obscuring a significant chunk of knowledge of the past.

As the taxi driver had predicted, tens of thousands of Cuencans of every age and social condition participated in the vigil that followed the beloved priest's death on a Friday until his funeral on Sunday. Carlo Crespi's enduring concern had been for the less fortunate in society. In his final illness, suffocating with pneumonia and his voice reduced to a whimper, he still repeated anxiously, *"No dejen llorar a los ninos. Donde esta el nino que llora? Ayuden a los ninos que sufren."* (Don't let the children cry. Where is there a child crying? Help the suffering children.) It is not as an antiquarian that Padre Crespi will be remembered in Ecuador, but as a saintly man, a pastor never too busy or too tired to attend to the needs of his humble flock.

BIBLIOGRAPHY

Besant, Annie, and Charles W. Leadbeater. *Man, Whence, How, and Whither.* Adyar: The Theosophical Press, 1913.

Cathie, Bruce. *The Energy Grid, Harmonic 695, The Pulse of the Universe.* Kempton, Ill.: Adventures Unlimited Press, 1997.

Childress, David Hatcher. *Lost Cities and Ancient Mysteries of South America.* Kempton, Ill.: Adventures Unlimited Press, 1988.

———. *Vimana Aircraft of Ancient India and Atlantis.* Kempton, Ill.: Adventures Unlimited Press, 1998.

Rig Veda. Selected, edited, and annotated by Wendy Doniger O'Flaherty. New York: Penguin Classics, 1981.

Shepherd, Aaron. *Savitri.* Park Ridge, Ill.: Albert Whitman and Company, 1992.

Sigma, Rho. *Ether Technology.* Kempton, Ill.: Adventures Unlimited Press, 1966.

Van Nooten, Barend A. *The Mahabharata.* New York: Twayne Publishers, 1971.

Zaehner, R. C. *Hindu Scriptures.* Edited by Dominic Godall. Berkeley: University of California Press, 1996.

INDEX

Page numbers in *italics* refer to figures.

2012, 103

Adams, Trig, 17
adhesives, 52–56, *53*, *55*, 87
Afghanistan, 49
Africa and Africans, 62
aircraft, 71–72, 92–95, 104–8
airplane crashes, 4–9, *6*
Alexander of Macedon, 99
Allies, 94–95
alphabet tablets, *pl.11*
Ampheres, 126
anacondas, 75
Ancient American, 61–62
Andhakas, 107
antigravity crafts, 71–72, 95
Aristotle, 82
Arjuna, 97, 110, 111
arks, 24, *24*

armor, *pl.3*, 23–24
army, million man, 79, 98
Arriaga, Jose de, 153
Artepracticas factory, 152, 153–54
Aryans, 96–97
Ashoka, King, 97–98
Asvattha-varm, 110–11
Asvin, 119
Atahualpa, 64–65, 99, 101, 102, 145
Athene, 137
Atlantis and Atlanteans, 76–77
   Besant on, 51–53, 56–57
   descriptions of, *pl.13*, 81–82, 116
   Ice Age and, 118–20
   legends of, 79–85
   location of, 79
   Mahabharata and, 96–102
   power of, 133–34
   See also Critias; diffusion; *Timaeus*

Atlantis fog, 16–17

"Atlantis in Peru, 12,000 BC," 51–53,
56–57

Atlantis: The Antediluvian World, 123,
135

Atlas, 126, 133

atomic weapons, 97–98, 104, 107–9,
111–12

    fictional account of, 114–17

    modern explosion of, 113–14

Augustine, 103–4

aurichalcum, 126, 129

Aurobindu Ghosh, Sri, 104

Bahamas bank, 10–16

Bahrata, 119

ballast, 16

balsa wood, 92–93

Barton, J. Golden, *pl.19*

Belzoni, 55

Berassi, Virgilio, 155

Berlitz, Charles, 158

Bermuda Triangle, 15

Besant, Annie, *pl.13,* 48–50, 77, 116,
121

    excerpts from "Atlantis in Peru,
12,000 BC," 51–53, 56–57

    opening of brow chakra, 49–50

    political causes of, 48–49

Bimini Islands Yacht Club, 4

"Bishop Freddie," 120–21

bison, 79

Blavatsky, Helena, 76–77

blower, 11, *12*

Bolivia, 74–75

Boroto, Richard, 146

Bosco, John, 146

Braun, Werner von, 94–95

Brazil, 74–75, 100

British Royal Geographical Society, 74

Brotherhood and Sisterhood of the
Saints, 50

brow chakra, 49–50

Brush, Bob, 17

Burrows, Herbert, 48–49

cannibalism, 116

Cardozo, Rene, 145

Cayce, Edgar, 87–88, 116

Central Bank Museum, 61–62, 67,
145, 148, 150–51, 159

Centro Cultural Abraham Lincoln,
146

Cheesman, Paul, 143, 157–58

child labor system, 48–49

Churchill, Winston, 94

Church of Maria Auxiliadora, 58–60

circles, 103

Clavijo, Ezequiel, 148–49

Cleghorn, Sarah Norcliffe, 49

Cleito, 125, 128

Cleopatra, 154

Coast Guard, U.S., 9

Cole, John, 143

Colegio Agronomica Salesiana, 152,
154

Colegio Cornelio Merchan, 148

Colegio Nacional Kleber Franco Cruz,
153

Colegio Orientalist Salesiano, 153

Communion of Ascended Saints,
50–51

Comus, King, *pl.8*, 64
conspiracies, 69–72
Cook, Elwood, 49–50
Cook, Warren, 28, 58, 62, 64, 142–60
Copernicus, 82
copper wheels, *52*, 52
Crespi, Carlo, 1, *pl.10*, *pl.16*, 17, *35*,
    39, *46*
  accomplishments of, 147–48
  death of, 142, 160
  deeper look at collection, 142–60
  diffusion and, 67–68
  doubts about judgment of, 158–59
  early life of, 146–47
  kind deeds of, 148–50
  sale of collection of, 58–66, 150–53
Crespi Collection, 17–18, *20–46*,
    20–47
  deeper look at, 142–60
  photographing of, 144, 158
  sale and cover-up of, 58–66, 150–53
Crespo (museum chief), 59, 67–68
Critias, 79–82, 123–34
crowns, *pl.3*, *pl.8*, 64
Crutchfield, James A., 113–14
Cuartel Cayambe, 152
Cuenca, Ecuador, 17, 19, 53–54, 60,
    143–44, 145, 148–49
Cueva de los Tayos, 150

Däniken, Erich von, 150
Darwin, Charles, 103–4
Davidovits, Joseph, 55
David plaque, 68, 154
Dayan, Moshe, 65
death, 51

Dexter, Warren, 58, 64, 142–60
diffusion, 47, 62, 67–68, 157
dinosaurs, 24, *42*
Diodorus Siculus, 82
Dona, Klaes, 62
Donnelly, Ignatius, 123, 135
doomsday device, 110–12
Drake, Francis, 62
Dropidas, 125, 135

Easter Island, 98, 108
Eguez, Cecelia de, 19–20
Eguez, Oswaldo, *35*, 35–36
Egyptians, colonization of Peru, 17
Elasippus, 126
electricity, 50
elephants, *27*, 158
El Molino, 53–54, *53–54*
El Panecillo, 86–91, *89–91*
energy, 50
Estan, 70–71
Euaemon, 126
Eumelus, 126
evolution, 57, 103–4

Fascists, 63
Fawcett, Jack, 77–78
Fawcett, Percy, 74–78
Fell, Barry, *pl.5*, 23, 62, 64, 142–43
Fer de Lance snakes, 75
fetishism, 149
Fimbul winter, 101, 118–21
Firestone of Atlantis, 88
flies, 75
Flores-Haro, Father, 28, 65–66, 148,
    149, 150, 152, 157, 159

flying ships, 92–95, 104–8
food, 56–57
foo fighters, 94
forgeries, 28–29, *30*, *42*, *44–45*, 47,
      148–50
"fossy jaw," 48
fountains, 129
Fox, Hugh, 154–55
Freddie, Bishop, 120–21
free energy, 50, 95
Fuller, Buckminster, 56
funguses, 75

Gadeirus, 126
Gama, Vasco de, 62
geodesic domes, 56
Ghurka people, 97–98
glue, 52–56, *53*, *55*, 87
gold, 29–30, 64–66. *See also* sheet metal
"Gold Links, The," 49
Gold of the Gods, The, 150
Goliath plaque, 68, 154
Gorbovsky, A., 114
Goya, Francisco de, 155
granite, 11, 16
Grann, David, 75
Granville, Joe, 16
Great Britain, child labor in, 48–49
Greece, 80
grinding mills, 24
guns, 99

Harappa, 112
Haviland, Geoffrey de, 93
helmets, *pl.19*, 23, *42*, 64
Hepburn, Charles, 144

Hermidia, Reinoso, 59, 63, 64, 151
Herodotus, 82
Heyerdal, Thor, 108
Hiddo, 83
Hindus and Hinduism, 57, 97–102
      fictional account of nuclear attack,
            114–17
      global war and, 110–12
      time and, 103–6
Hitler, Adolf, 94
Holm, Olaf, 59, 63, 64, 151
Hoomi, Koot, 49–50, 121
Huascar, 101
Huayna Capac, 101–2, 145
humidity, 75
hurricanes, 12

Ice Age, 116, 118–20
IFOs, 93, 110
ihenni flies, 75
Inca Pirca, *54*
Incas, 101–2, 143–44
India, 49, 96–97, 101
Indian National Congress, 49
interdimensional seeing, 121
Interpretation of Radium, The, 104
It Happened in New Mexico, 113–14

Johnson, Doris, 11
Joseph, Chief, 79
joy, 51
Junior, 16
Jupiter, 121

Kon-Tiki, 108
Krantor, 82

Krishna, 97, 110, 111
Kukulkan, 143

Laithwaite, Eric, 93, 95
La Olla, *90–91*
laser, prehistoric, 86–91, *89–91*
launch mantra, 111
Leadbeater, Charles Webster, 49, 121
Letters of the Masters of the Wisdom,
    121
Leukippe, 125
Lopez, Michael, 4–5, *14*
Lost City of Z, The, 75
Lova, Pedro, 59–61, 64, 67, 156
Lowenstein, Kurt, *pl.18*

machinery, 51–52, *52*
maggots, 74–75
magnetite, 16–17
Mahabharata, 92, 96–102
    flying ships and, 104–6
    global war and, 110–12
maha chohan, 50
maize, 56
Malo, Benigno, 157
Man, Whence, How, and Whither, 50,
    51–53, 56–57, 77
Manetho the Mendesian, 82
Manoa, 76
marble blocks, 12
marble temple, 10–15, *13*
Masinissa Plaque, 143, 157–58
Mato Grosso, 76, 78
May, Wayne, 61–62, 66
Mayans, 62
Mayol, Jacques, 16

Melville, Herman, 122
Memory, 123
mercury-powered aircraft, 106–8
Mestor, 126
Midwestern Epigraphic Society, 62
milk, 56
Mneseus, 126
Mohenjo Daro, 96, 98, 108, 111–12,
    113–14
Monteith, Henry, 106–7
Moreno, Gabriel Garcia, 159–60
Morgan, J. P., 50–51
Moricz, Juan, 150
Moseley, Beverly, 142
Mosquito bomber, 92–93
motorcycles, 99
mounds. *See* El Panecillo
mummy cases, 65
Museo del Banco Central, 61–62, 67,
    145, 148, 150–51, 159
Museo Nacional de Antropología, 62

natural disasters, 83–84
Nazis, 63
Nigeria, 62
Nine Just Men, 98, 121
Nisrochs, *pl.12*, 29, 31–32, 47, 154
nuclear weapons, 97–98, 104, 107–9,
    111–12
    fictional account of, 114–17
    modern explosion of, 113–14

Occult Chemistry, 49–50
Oera Linda Boek, 82–85, 116, 118–19
Okke, 83
Olcott, Henry, 104

Old Masters, 155
Oppenheimer, J. Robert, 104–5
Over de Linden, Cornelius, 83

Pachacuti the Fourth, 101
paintings, 63, 155
Pakarati, 108
Pakistan, 111–12
Panecillo, Ecuador, 86–91, *89–91*
pencil winds, 15–16
Pillars of Hercules, 80, 124, 140
Pioneer, 121
Pizzaro, Francisco, 65, 101–2
plaques, *pl.1*, *pl.2*, *pl.16*, *pl.21*, *pl.22*,
    24, 29, 31–32, *31–33*, 68
Plato, 79–82, 98, 123–34
Poseidon, 125–26, 128, 132–33
potatoes, 56
power, 50, 95
Practicas, Atresanias, 63
Pranadhara, 107
Psonchis, 80–82
Puma Pongo, 145, 159

Quetzalcoatl, 143
Quipu, 101
Quiteno tribe, 87
Quito, Ecuador, 86–87

Rajyadhara, 107
Rasmussen, Donald, 144
red race, 79
Reinosa, Gustavo, 157
religion, 51
Revista Anthropologico, 67–68
rice, 56

Richardson, Jim, 10, *13*, 14–16
Richardson, Robbie, 10–11
Riddles in Ancient History, 114
rifles, 99
Rig Veda, 106
Rimmell, Raleigh, 77–78
Rio Xingu, 76
Roman arches, 87
Rongorongo writing, 98, 108, 112

*Sage America: A Startling New Theory
    on the Old World Settlement of
    America before Columbus,* 143
Salcedo, Carlos Ramirez, 149
Salesian order, 60
Sama Negara Sutradara, 106
San Andres Mountains, 113–14
Schauberger, Viktor, 93–94
Schwartz, Jean-Michel, 98
Searle, John, 93, 95
Secret Doctrine, The, 77, 121
Secrets of Easter Island, The, 98
Segundo (worker), *34*
Serra do Roncador, 76
Serrano, Alfonso, 144, 145
shale, 16
Shaw, George Bernard, 49
sheet metal, *pl.5*, *pl.6*, *pl.18*, *pl.19*, 24,
    28, *29*, 56, 67–68
ship's ballast, 16
Sinnett, A. P., 121
skeletons, radioactive, 108, 112, 114
Skene, Edward, 8
smugglers, 4–9
snakes, 75
Socrates, 123, 135

Soddy, Frederick, 104
Solon, 80–82, 124, 136–39
step pyramids, 64
Stone Age, 119–20
suicide, 51
sun, 51
sweetmeats, 56–57

Tapuyas, 76
technology, 86–91, 97–98
Terranova, Hector, 58
Tesla, Nikola, 50
Theosophical Society, 49, 104
Timaeus, 135–41
time, 103–6
tin, 12
Toral, Hernan Crespo, 157
Trinity Site, 112, 113–14
trout, 93–94
tunnels, 70–71, 87–88, 150
Turolla, Pino, 155, 156
Twiskland, 84

UFOs, 92–95
universal force, 50

Valdivia Period, 151
Valentine, Manson, 14, 17, 158
vampire bats, 75
Vatican, 65–66
vayu, 106–7

Verwijs, E., 83
vimanas, 92, 107
Vitringa, J. R., 83
volcanos, 86
Vrishnis, 107

Wade, Cory, 55
wallpaper, 56, 67–68. *See also* sheet metal
Walters Art Gallery, 29, 46–47
Westland, 84
wheels, *52*
winds, 15–16
Wingate, Beatrice, 8
Wingate, Mike, 11, 69–71
Wingate, Richard, 4–9, *7, 9, pl.10, 20*
   exploring the Crespi Collection, *20–46,* 20–47
   visits with Crespi, *pl.10,* 19–20, *20,* 68
winter, Fimbul, 118–20
wireless transmission, 50
wooden UFOs, 92–95
World Age, 103
World War II, 94–95
wrecks, surrounding marble temple, 11–14

yams, 56
Yniguez, Juan Cordero, 150

Zeus, 134

BOOKS OF RELATED INTEREST

Atlantis and 2012
The Science of the Lost Civilization and the Prophecies of the Maya
by Frank Joseph

Survivors of Atlantis
Their Impact on World Culture
by Frank Joseph

Atlantis and the Kingdom of the Neanderthals
100,000 Years of Lost History
by Colin Wilson

Atlantis and the Cycles of Time
Prophecies, Traditions, and Occult Revelations
by Joscelyn Godwin

The Lost Civilization of Lemuria
The Rise and Fall of the World's Oldest Culture
by Frank Joseph

The Destruction of Atlantis
Compelling Evidence of the Sudden Fall of the Legendary Civilization
by Frank Joseph

Forbidden History
Prehistoric Technologies, Extraterrestrial Intervention,
and the Suppressed Origins of Civilization
Edited by J. Douglas Kenyon

Forbidden Science
From Ancient Technologies to Free Energy
Edited by J. Douglas Kenyon

INNER TRADITIONS • BEAR & COMPANY
P.O. Box 388
Rochester, VT 05767
1-800-246-8648
www.InnerTraditions.com

Or contact your local bookseller